Birds Among the Stanzas

An Anthology

Compiled By

Joy Viola Simons

Watermark Press

Birds Among the Stanzas

Library of Congress
Cataloging in Publication Data
ISBN 1-56167-013-8

Published by
Watermark Press
11-J Gwynns Mill Court
Owings Mills, Maryland 21117

Manufactured in the United States of America

TO
MY MOTHER
Vivian V. Simons
My Inspiration
This book is lovingly dedicated

CONTENTS

CONTENTS

Crow

Cuckoo

Dove

Eagle

Goldfinch

Humming-Bird

Lark

CONTENTS

CONTENTS

CONTENTS

Introduction

Little bird, fly down near to me
From your throne on the branch of the tree,
Let your throat send forth song
Like the music of dreams,
While your feathers prolong
With their hues beauty's beams;
Little bird, do stay near me a while -
You're a friend with a nod that's a smile.

I composed these lines one day when I had been thinking about birds that I had seen, and when I had been recollecting poems that I had read, poems which either merely mention birds, or which have birds as their principal themes.

Birds of various kinds and sizes have been active and popular inhabitants of the world for many hundreds of years. Before word-poems were recorded, birds appeared in a variety of art forms. After recorded writing arrived, and from then on into the twentieth century, birds have been favorite and fascinating subjects for human beings to select as vehicles for their artistic outlets.

Following are five examples of birds in art forms other than writing. These examples provide both historical and comparative perspectives within which to place the written word -- poems by poets whom scholars designate as either major or minor contributors to literary written art.

1) Peacock or Cock; 9th century B.C., Greek. The Metropolitan Museum of Art. Sculpture, of metal.
2) Magpie on a Flowering Branch; c. 960-1279, Chinese. The Metropolitan Museum of Art. A painting.
3) Owl; 1508, by Albrecht Durer, German. Albertina, Vienna. A painting.
4) Eagle's Wing; 1512, by Albrecht Durer, German. Albertina, Vienna. A painting.
5) Landscape with Blue Birds; 1919, by Paul Klee. Philadelphia Museum of Art. A painting.

Written poems which mention or emphasize birds, are generally as pictorially descriptive as the various other artform manifestations -- provided human beings permit themselves to visualize each written idea, and to examine between the poetry lines with an intuitive comprehension that can and will grasp the intended images of the birds enthroned among the stanzas. Such visualization and examination offer to human beings an opportunity to identify with birds in a number of ways, and to receive from birds an association that is not quite so possible with other of earth's objects. Birds are small, winged and feathered, but here, figuratively speaking, do the contrasts end. Birds and humans possess in differing quantities and in accordance with individuality, as each moves within its own mobile world, varying yet similar characteristics. For instance, there are degrees of beauty, of ordinary appearance, of ugliness; there are actions of bravery; there are attitudes of aloofness and contentment. Some humans are powerful and swift as eagles, while others are gentle and loving as doves. Some humans prefer the darkness to light,as the owl, and some accept sacrifice nobly, as the tiny goldfinch lives its days. Many humans chatter like sparrows, and feel as defensively lowly. Some birds are destructive and violent and do not operate as

1

though life were precious. This is typified in the nursery tale which presents the sparrow in the role of the villain:

> "Who killed Cock Robin?"
> "I," said the sparrow -
> "With my bow and arrow."

And to quote William Blake:

> "He who shall hurt the little wren
> Shall never be beloved by men."

Anatole France declared that "music is an art common to men and birds." While not all people are Beethovens, neither are all birds nightingales.

Today, amidst ever-present and consuming turmoils and concerns, I like to believe that birds can function as sources of personal peace. As we human beings exist through our hours in a world saturated with technology, prejudices and generation gaps, from which we tend to lack imagination, tolerance and cooperation, we desperately need some recurring sources of personal peace. Human beings can be adaptable, but often times become so victimized that they are unable to perform in suitable, stable directions. They need frequent, overpowering signs of change, harmony, grace, hope. Birds can never supply ultimate answers nor final solutions, but birds can be on-going sources for reaffirming the joys of living life within expected bounds, of flying freely through daily duties and pleasures, always mindful that with every decision made thereby hinges the outcomes of either rebellion or repose. Birds know nothing of mankind's races, religions, economic situations -- all three of which are besetting human beings today. Consequently no conflicts can arise from birds to human beings, from human beings to birds, or between birds and human beings, because of problems which all too often do occur from these circumstances. Human beings can identify with birds because human beings can be assured that no barriers exist between human beings and birds, and with this assurance can come the opportunities for human beings to obtain from birds comforting friendships, unbiased outlooks, escape from self-centeredness, attractive and unaffected ways -- to help in the enrichment of their human lives, and in contributing toward the calming of their emotions and the establishing of some elements of peace within their hearts. Birds have the powers to provide this for human beings. To be aware of birds, to watch birds, to get to know birds as friends, to read about birds -- can bring to human beings an awakening of external interests, deeper understandings, truer beauties, relaxing attitudes, generous behaviors.

With these several ideas in mind, I created this anthology of poetry about birds, hoping as I selected each poem, that messages toward personal peace would be forthcoming to every reader.

The poems which I have chosen are by poets from both England and the United States. The poems present similarities, parallels and differences.

I hope that in reading this anthology in its entirety or in parts, that each reader will realize and will subsequently accept the meanings that are inherent, the messages that are there. I hope that each reader will decide to begin to let little birds stay nearby for a while, not necessarily in a literal, physical sense, but at least in a figurative, mental sense, and that in so doing the reader will ponder the thought that all robins are robins, all robins are birds, all human beings are human beings. There are many kinds of birds upon the earth -- there

2

are many kinds of human beings upon the earth. The medieval saint and mystic, St. Francis of Assisi, often spoke to the birds (especially to the larks which were his favorites), and he blessed the birds, filled deeply as he always was with kindness and with joy. He looked upon the whole of mankind as a single family, and he maintained that a person's daily stresses should not stop the recognizing of beauty. Birds and people were his great concerns.

Cannot our looking at a bird soaring across the sky, or cannot the attuning of our ears to a chirping bird outside our window, bring a respite from our pressures, or give a touch of beauty to encourage our exhausted hearts? I think these to be possible, if we only allow ourselves to acknowledge and to accept the opportunities that are available from the warm-blooded, vertebrate beings of birds -- whether they be in reality, in writing, or in some other kind of art form manifestation.

From this anthology, beginning with poems about the albatross and ending with poems about the wren, may every reader be lifted above and away from discouragement and from feelings of failure -- high to the heights of encouragement and feelings of optimism. This is my wish -- a wish which is excellently expressed by Victor Hugo in his poem entitled "Be Like the Bird":

"Be like the bird, who
Halting in his flight
On limb too slight
Feels it give way beneath him,
Yet sings
Knowing he hath wings."

Albatross

The Albatross

by Charles Baudelaire; translated by Francis Duke

For entertainment, sailors sometimes take
The albatross, that great sea-bird who sweeps
Across the sky, slow consort in the wake
Of vessels moving on the rolling deep.

Thrown on the deck, the king of azure sky,
Ashamed to know that he no longer soars,
Drags at his sides, disheveled and awry,
His great white wings, bent back like trailing oars.

How gauche, that winged voyager, and how weak!
Just now so fair, how ugly and absurd!
One tries to thrust a pipe into his beak;
Another limps, to mock the grounded bird!

The Poet, like that monarch of the clouds,
To arrow and to storm alike defiant,
Exiled on earth among the jeering crowds,
Walks awkwardly because his wings are giant.

Albatross

from "The Rhime of the Ancient Mariner"
by Samuel Taylor Coleridge

"The ice was here, the ice was there,
The ice was all around:
It cracked and growled, and roared and howled,
Like noises in a swound.

At length did cross an Albatross;
Through the fog it came;
As if it had been a Christian soul,
We hailed it in God's name.

It ate the food it ne'er had eat,
And round and round it flew.
The ice did split with a thunder-fit;
The helmsman steered us through!

And a good south wind sprung up behind;
The Albatross did follow,
And every day, for food or play,
Came to the mariners' hollo!

In mist or cloud, on mast or shroud,
It perched for vespers nine;
Whiles all the night, through fog-smoke white,
Glimmered the white moon-shine."

"God save thee, ancient mariner,
From the fiends, that plague thee thus! -
Why look'st thou so?" - "With my cross-bow
I shot the Albatross.

The Sun now rose upon the right:
Out of the sea came he,
Still hid in mist, and on the left
Went down into the sea.

And the good south wind still blew behind,
But no sweet bird did follow,
Nor any day for food or play
Came to the mariners' hollo!

And I had done a hellish thing,
And it would work 'em woe;
For all averred, I had killed the bird
That made the breeze to blow.
Ah wretch! said they, the bird to slay,
That made the breeze to blow!

Nor dim nor red, like God's own head,
The glorious Sun uprist.
Then all averred, I had killed the bird
That brought the fog and mist.
'Twas right, said they, such birds to slay,
That bring the fog and mist.

The fair breeze blew, the white foam flew,
The furrow followed free;
We were the first that ever burst
Into that silent sea.

Down dropt the breeze, the sails dropt down,
'Twas sad as sad could be;
And we did speak only to break
The silence of the sea!

All in a hot and copper sky,
The bloody Sun, at noon,
Right up above the mast did stand,
No bigger than the Moon.

Day after day, day after day,
We stuck, nor breath nor motion;
As idle as a painted ship
Upon a painted ocean.

Water, water, everywhere,
And all the boards did shrink;
Water, water, everywhere,
Nor any drop to drink.

The very deep did rot: O Christ!
That ever this Should be!
Yea, slimy things did crawl with legs
Upon the slimy sea.

Albatross (cont'd)

About, about, in reel and rout
The death-fires danced at night;
The water, like a witch's oils,
Burnt green, and blue, and white.

And some in dreams assured were
Of the spirit that plagued us so:
Nine fathom deep he had followed us
From the land of mist and snow.

And every tongue, through utter drought,
Was withered at the root;
We could not speak, no more than if
We had been choked with soot.

Ah, well-a-day! what evil looks
Had I from old and young!
Instead of the cross, the Albatross
About, my neck was hung.

Albatross

by Charles Warren Stoddard

Time cannot age thy sinews, nor the gale
Batter the network of thy feathered mail,
Lone sentry of the deep!
Among the crashing caverns of the storm,
With wing unfettered, lo! thy frigid form
Is whirled in dreamless sleep!

Where shall thy wing find rest for all its might?
Where shall thy lidless eye, that scours the night,
Grow blank in utter death?
When shall thy thousand years have stripped thee bare,
Invulnerable spirit of the air,
And sealed thy giant-breath?

Not till thy bosom hugs the icy wave, -
Not till thy palsied limbs sink in that grave,
Caught by the shrieking blast,
And hurled upon the sea with broad wings locked,
On an eternity of waters rocked,
Defiant to the last!

Blackbird

Sing a Song of Sixpence

Mother Goose

Sing a song of sixpence,
A pocket full of rye;
Four-and-twenty blackbirds,
Baked in a pie.

When the pie was opened,
The birds began to sing;
Was not that a dainty dish,
To set before the king?

The king was in his counting-house,
Counting out his money;
The queen was in the parlor,
Eating bread and honey.

The maid was in the garden,
Hanging out the clothes;
Down came a blackbird,
And pecked off her nose.

From A Winter's Day

by Joanna Baillie.

But at a distance, on the leafless tree,
All woe-begone, the lonely blackbird sits;
The cold north wind ruffles his glossy feathers;
Full oft he looks, but dares not make approach,
Then turns his yellow beak to peck his side
And claps his wings close to his sharpen'd breast.
The wandering fowler from behind the hedge,
Fastens his eye upon him, points his gun,
And firing wantonly, as at a mark,
Of life bereaves him in the cheerful spot
That oft hath echo'd to his summer's song.

Vespers

by Thomas Edward Brown

O blackbird, what a boy you are!
How you do go it!
Blowing your bugle to that one sweet star -
How you do blow it!
And does she hear you, blackbird boy, so far?
Or is it wasted breath?
"Good Lord! She is so bright
To-night!"
The blackbird saith.

The Blackbird

by William Ernest Henley

The nightingale has a lyre of gold,
The lark's is a clarion call,
And the blackbird plays but a boxwood flute,
But I love him best of all.

For his song is all of the joy of life,
And we in the mad, spring weather,
We two have listened till he sang
Our hearts and lips together.

12

The Blackbird

by Alfred Tennyson

A Blackbird! sing me something well:
While all the neighbors shoot thee round,
I keep smooth plats of fruitful ground,
Where thou may'st warble, eat, and dwell.

The espaliers and the standards all
Are thine; the range of lawn and park.
The unnetted black-hearts ripen dark,
All thine, against the garden wall.

Yet, tho' I spared ye all the spring,
Thy sole delight is, sitting still,
With that gold dagger of thy bill
To fret the summer jenneting.

A golden bill! the silver tongue,
Cold February loved, is dry:
Plenty corrupts the melody
That made thee famous once, when young.

And in the sultry garden-squares,
Now thy flute-notes are changed to coarse,
I hear thee not at all, or hoarse
As when a hawker hawks his wares.

Take warning! he that will not sing
While yon sun prospers in the blue,
Shall sing for want, ere leaves are new,
Caught in the frozen palms of Spring.

Verses on Seeing the Destruction of a Blackbird's Nest

by James Walker

What sad destruction's this I see
Within the hoary hawthorn tree;
Oh! blasted be his cruel e'e
And savage breast,
What tore, in wanton cruelty,
This bonnie nest.

Here on the boughs, wi' blossoms fringed,
The parent pair it snugly hinged;
For moss and twigs how fond they ranged
The woodlands green,
Till Sol in setting glory tinged
The clouds at e'en.

As day by day unhalting flew,
Their little fabric larger grew,
Snug lined wi' hair and flakes o' woo;
And soon there lay
Five spatted eggs o' greeny blue
In bright display.

Then true to Nature's simple law,
The hen-bird nestled on them a',
Soon wi' a mither's pride she saw
Five nestling's nude -
The pride, the pleasure of the shaw
And leafy wood.

And while she sat as gloamin' lower'd,
Her faithful sable-plumaged lord
Sat perched among the boughs embower'd
Wi' blossoms fair,
And rich his gushing music poured,
And soothed her care.

Her little minstrels thrave and grew,
She quenched their thirst wi' blobs o' dew
That hung frae ilka thorny bough
At morning grey,
And brocht them writhing worms enow
Ilk passing day.

Verses on Seeing the Destruction of a Blackbird's Nest (cont'd)

But time wheel'd roond the evil hour
Which brocht the spoiler's ruthless pow'r,
He forth the nest exulting tore,
Sae neatly hung,
And off in savage triumph bore
The helpless young.

Then blasted are their hopes and joys,
And severed are a parent's ties,
And here a' wrecked and ruined lies
Their dear-loved hame,
Which a' the boast of art defies
To frame the same.

Bluebird

The Bluebird

by John Banister Tabb

When God had made a host of them,
One little flower still lacked a stem
To hold its blossom blue;
So into it He breathed a song,
And suddenly, with petals strong
As wings, away it flew.

The Bluebird

by James Maurice Thompson

When ice is thawed and snow is gone,
And racy sweetness floods the trees;
When snow-birds from the hedge have flown,
And on the hive-porch swarm the bees, -
Drifting down the first warm wind
That thrills the earliest days of spring,
The bluebird seeks our maple groves,
And charms them into tasseling.

He sits among the delicate sprays,
With mists of splendor round him drawn,
And through the spring's prophetic veil
Sees summer's rich fulfillment dawn:
He sings, and his is nature's voice, -
A gush of melody sincere
From that great fount of harmony
Which thaws and runs when spring is here.

Short is his song, but strangely sweet
To ears aweary of the low,
Dull tramp of winter's sullen feet,
Sandaled in ice and muffed in snow:
Short is his song, but through it runs
A hint of dithyrambs yet to be, -
A sweet suggestiveness that has
The influence of prophecy.

From childhood I have nursed a faith
In bluebird's songs and winds of spring:
They tell me after frost and death
There comes a time of blossoming;
And after snow and cutting sleet,
The cold, stern mood of nature yields
To tender warmth, when bare pink feet
Of children press her greening fields.

Sing strong and clear, O bluebird dear!
While all the land with splendor fills,
While maples gladden in the vales,
And plum-trees blossom on the hills:
Float down the wind on shining wings,
And do thy will by grove and stream,
While through my life spring's freshness runs
Like music through a poet's dream.

The Bluebirds

by Henry David Thoreau

In the midst of the poplar that stands by our door,
We planted a bluebird box,
And we hoped before the summer was o'er
A transient pair to coax.

One warm summer's day the bluebirds came
And lighted on our tree,
But at first the wand'rers were not so tame
But they were afraid of me.

They seemed to come from the distant south,
Just over the Walden wood,
And they skimmed it along with open mouth
Close by where the bellows stood.

Warbling they swept round the distant cliff,
And they warbled it over the lea,
And over the blacksmith's shop in a jiff
Did they come warbling to me.

They came and sat on the box's top
Without looking into the hole,
And only from this side to that did they hop,
As 'twere a common well-pole.

Methinks I had never seen them before,
Nor indeed had they seen me,
Till I chanced to stand by our back door,
And they came to the poplar tree.

In course of time they built their nest
And reared a happy brood,
And every morn they piped their best
As they flew away to the wood.

Thus wore the summer hours away
To the bluebirds and to me,
And every hour was a summer's day,
So pleasantly lived we.

They were a world within themselves,
And I a world in me,
Up in the tree - the little elves -
With their callow family.

The Bluebirds (cont'd)

One morn the wind blowed cold and strong,
And the leaves when whirling away;
The birds prepared for their journey long
That raw and gusty day.

Boreas came blust'ring down from the north,
And ruffled their azure smocks,
So they launched them forth, thought somewhat loth,
By way of the old Cliff rocks.

Meanwhile the earth jogged steadily on
In her mantle of purest white,
And anon another spring was born
When winter was vanished quite.

And I wandered forth o'er the steamy earth,
And gazed at the mellow sky,
But never before from the hour of my birth
Had I wandered so thoughtfully.

For never before was the earth so still,
And never so mild was the sky,
The river, the fields, the woods, and the hill,
Seemed to heave an audible sigh.

I felt that the heavens were all around,
And the earth was all below,
As when in the ears there rushes a sound
Which thrills you from top to toe.

I dreamed that I was an waking thought -
A something I hardly knew -
Not a solid peace, nor an empty nought,
But a drop of morning dew.

'Twas the world and I at a game of bo-peep,
As a man would dodge his shadow,
An idea becalmed in eternity's deep -
'Tween Lima and Segraddo.

Anon a faintly warbled note
From out the azure deep,
Into my ears did gently float
As is the approach of sleep.

The Bluebirds (cont'd)

It thrilled but startled not my soul;
Across my mind strange mem'ries gleamed,
As often distant scenes unroll
When we have lately dreamed.

The bluebird had come from the distant South
To his box in the poplar tree,
And he opened wide his slender mouth,
On purpose to sing to me.

The American Bluebird

by Alexander Wilson

When winter's cold tempests and snows are no more,
Green meadows and brown-furrowed fields re-appearing,
The fishermen hauling their shad to the shore,
And cloud-cleaving geese to the lakes are a-steering,
When first the lone butterfly flits on the wing,
When red grow the maples, so fresh and so pleasing,
O then comes the Blue-Bird, the herald of spring!
And hails with his warblings the charms of the season.

Then loud piping frogs make the marshes to ring;
Then warm glows the sunshine, and fine is the weather;
The blue woodland flowers just beginning to spring,
And spicewood and sassafras budding together;
O then to your gardens, ye housewives, repair!
Your walks border up; sow and plant at your leisure;
The Blue-Bird will chaunt from his box such an air,
That all your hard toils will seem truly a pleasure.

He flits through the orchard, he visits each tree,
The red flowering peach and the apples' sweet blossoms;
He snaps up destroyers wherever they be,
And seizes the caitiffs that lurk in their bosoms;
He drags the vile grub from the corn it devours,
The worms from their webs, where they riot and welter;
His song and his services freely are ours,
And all that he asks is in summer a shelter.

The ploughman is pleased when he gleans in his train,
Now searching the furrows, - now mounting to cheer him;
The gardener delights in his sweet simple strain,
And leans on his spade to survey and to hear him;
The slow lingering school-boys forget they'll be chid,
While gazing intent as he warbles before 'em,
In mantle of sky-blue, and bosom so red,
That each little loiterer seems to adore him.

When all the gay scenes of the summer are o'er,
And autumn slow enters, so silent and sallow,
And millions of warblers, that charmed us before,
Have fled in the train of the sun-seeking swallow;
The Blue-Bird, forsaken, yet true to his home,
Still lingers, and looks for a milder tomorrow,
Till forced by the horrors of winter to roam,
He sings his adieu in a lone note of sorrow.

The American Blue-Bird (cont'd)

While spring's lovely season, serene, dewy, warm,
The green face of earth, and the pure blue of heaven,
Or love's native music have influence to charm,
Or sympathy's glow to our feelings are given;
Still dear to each bosom the Blue-Bird shall be;
His voice, like the thrillings of hope, is a treasure;
For through bleakest storms, if a calm he but see,
He comes to remind us of sunshine and pleasure!

Blue Jay

The Blue Jay

by Eben Pearson Dorr

The jay, he sings a scanty lay,
As boy who would a fiddle play,
Strikes one bar from tuneful harp,
Then screeches into discord sharp.
Though boy to task again can turn,
The bird, alas, may never learn.
Creator placed within his throat
A song that is a single note,
Yet sweet this mellow minor chord,
Prelude, perhaps it pleased the Lord,
To song reserved for other shore,
Now vaguely hinted - nothing more.

The Blue Jay

by Hamlin Garland

His eye is bright as burnished steel,
His note a quick defiant cry;
Harsh as a hinge his grating squeal
Sounds from the keen wind sweeping by.

Rains never dim his smooth blue coat,
The winter never troubles him.
No fog puts hoarseness in his throat,
Or makes his merry eyes grow dim.
His cry at morning is a shout,
His wing is subject to his heart.
Of fear he knows not - doubt
Did not draw his sailing chart.

He is an universal emigre;
His foot is set in every land.
He greets me by gray Casco bay,
And laughs across the Texas sand.
In heat or cold, in storm or sun
He lives unfearingly, and when he dies
He folds his feet up one by one
And turns a last look at the skies.

He is the true American! he fears
No journey and no wood or wall;
And in the desert, toiling voyagers
Take heart of courage from his call.

Bobolink

To the Lapland Longspur

by John Burroughs (Unalaska, July 18, 1899)

Oh, thou northland bobolink,
Looking over Summer's brink
Up to Winter, worn and dim,
Peering down from mountain rim,
Something takes me in thy tone,
Quivering wing, and bubbling throat;
Something moves me in thy ways -
Bird, rejoicing in thy days,
In thy upward-hovering flight.
In thy suit of black and white,
Chestnut cape and circled crown,
In thy mate of speckled brown;
Surely I may pause and think
Of my boyhood's bobolink.

Soaring over meadows wild
(Greener pastures never smiled);
Raining music from above,
Full of rapture, full of love;
Frolic, gay and debonair,
Yet not all exempt from care,
For thy nest is in the grass,
And thou worriest as I pass:
But nor hand nor foot of mine
Shall do harm to thee or thine;
I, musing, only pause to think
Of my boyhood's bobolink.

But no bobolink of mine
Ever sang o'er mead so fine,
Starred with flowers of every hue,
Gold and purple, white and blue;
Painted-cup, anemone,
Jacob's-ladder, fleur-de-lis,
Orchid, harebell, shooting-star,
Crane's-bill, lupine, seen afar,
Primrose, poppy, saxifrage,
Pictured type on Nature's page -
These and others here unnamed,
In northland gardens, yet untamed,
Deck the fields where thou dost sing,
Mounting up on trembling wing;
While in wistful mood I think
Of my boyhood's bobolink.

To the Lapland Longspur (cont'd)

On Unalaska's emerald lea,
On lonely isles in Bering Sea,
On far Siberia's barren shore,
On north Alaska's tundra floor,
At morn, at noon, in pallid night,
We heard thy song and saw thy flight,
While I, sighing, could but think
Of my boyhood's bobolink.

The Bobolink

by Thomas Hill

Bobolink! that in the meadow,
Or beneath the orchard's shadow,
Keepest up a constant rattle,
Joyous as my children's prattle,
Welcome to the north again!
Welcome to mine ear thy strain,
Welcome to mine eye the sight
Of thy buff, thy black and white!
Brighter plumes may greet the sun
By the banks of Amazon;
Sweeter tones may weave the spell
Of enchanting Philomel;
But the tropic bird would fail,
And the English nightingale,
If we should compare their worth
With thy endless, gushing mirth.

When the ides of May are past,
June and summer nearing fast,
While from depths of blue above
Comes the mighty breath of love,
Calling out each bud and flower
With resistless, secret power, -
Waking hope and fond desire,
Kindling the erotic fire, -
Filling youths' and maidens' dreams
With mysterious, pleasing themes, -
Then, amid the sunlight clear
Floating in the fragrant air,
Thou dost fill each heart with pleasure
By thy glad ecstatic measure.

A single note, so sweet and low,
Like a full heart's overflow,
Forms the prelude; but the strain
Gives us no such tone again,
For the wild and saucy song
Leaps and skips the notes among,
With such quick and sportive play,
Ne'er was madder, merrier lay.

The Bobolink (cont'd)

Gayest songster of the Spring!
Thy melodies before me bring
Visions of some dream-built land,
Where, by constant zephyrs fann'd,
I might walk the livelong day,
Embosom'd in perpetual May.
Nor care nor fear thy bosom knows;
For thee a tempest never blows;
But when our northern Summer's o'er,
By Delaware's or Schuylkill's shore
The wild rice lifts its airy head,
And royal feasts for thee are spread.
And when the winter threatens there,
Thy tireless wings yet own no fear,
But bear thee to more Southern coasts,
Far beyond the reach of frosts.

Bobolink! still may thy gladness
Take from me all taints of sadness;
Fill my soul with trust unshaken
In that Being who has taken
Care for every living thing,
In Summer, Winter, Fall and Spring.

The Bob O' Linkum

by Charles Fenno Hoffman

Thou vocal sprite! thou feather'd troubadour!
In pilgrim weeds through many a clime a ranger,
Comest thou to doff thy russet suit once more,
And play in foppish trim the masquing stranger?
Philosophers may teach thy whereabouts and nature;
But, wise as all of us, perforce, must think 'em,
The schoolboy best hath fix'd thy nomenclature,
And poets too must call thee Bob O' Linkum!

Say! art thou, long 'mid forest glooms benighted,
So glad to skim our laughing meadows over,
With our gay orchards here so much delighted,
It makes thee musical, thou airy rover?
Or are those buoyant notes the pilfer'd treasure
Of fairy isles, which thou hast learn'd to ravish
Of all their sweetest minstrelsy at pleasure,
And, Ariel-like, again on men to lavish?

They tell sad stories of thy mad-cap freaks;
Wherever o'er the land thy pathway ranges,
And even in a brace of wandering weeks,
They say, alike thy song and plumage changes:
Here both are gay; and when the buds put forth,
And leafy June is shading rock and river,
Thou art unmatch'd, blithe warbler of the north!
When through the balmy air thy clear notes quiver.

Joyous, yet tender, was that gush of song
Caught from the brooks, where, 'mid its wildflowers smiling,
The silent prairie listens all day long,
The only captive to such sweet beguiling;
Or didst thou, flitting through the verdurous halls
And column'd aisles of western groves symphonious,
Learn from the tuneful woods rare madrigals,
To make our flowering pastures here harmonious?

Caught'st thou thy carol from Otawa maid,
Where, through the liquid fields of wild rice plashing,
Brushing the ears from off the burden'd blade,
Her birch canoe o'er some lone lake is flashing?
Or did the reeds of some savannah south
Detain thee while thy northern flight pursuing,
To place those melodies in thy sweet mouth
The spice-fed winds had taught them in their wooing?

The Bob O' Linkum (cont'd)

Unthrifty prodigal! is thought of ill
Thy ceaseless roundelay disturbing ever?
Or doth each pulse in choiring cadence still
Throb on in music till at rest forever?
Yet, now in wilder'd maze of concord floating,
'Twould seem that glorious hymning to prolong,
Old Time, in hearing thee, might fall a doting,
And pause to listen to thy rapturous song!

Bobolink (Biglow Papers)

by James Russell Lowell

June's bridesman, poet o' the year,
Gladness on wings, the bobolink is here;
Half-hid in tip-top apple-blooms he swings,
Or climbs aginst the breeze with quiverin' wings,
Or, givin' way to 't in a mock despair,
Runs down, a brook o' laughter, thru the air.

Cardinal

The Cardinal Bird

by William Davis Gallagher

A day and then a week passed by:
The redbird hanging from the sill
Sang not; and all were wondering why
It was so still -
Then one bright morning, loud and clear,
Its whistle smote my drowsy ear,
Ten times repeated, till the sound
Filled every echoing niche around;
And all things earliest loved by me, -
The bird, the brook, the flower, the tree, -
Came back again, as thus I heard
The cardinal bird.

Where maple orchards towered aloft,
And spicewood bushes spread below,
Where skies were blue, and winds were soft,
I could but go -
For, opening through a wildering haze,
Appeared my restless childhood's days;
And truant feet and loitering mood
Soon found me in the same old wood
(Illusion's hour but seldom brings
So much the very form of things)
Where first I sought, and saw, and heard
The cardinal bird.

Then came green meadows, broad and bright,
Where dandelions, with wealth untold,
Gleamed on the young and eager sight
Like stars of gold;
And on the very meadow's edge,
Beneath the ragged blackberry hedge,
Mid mosses golden, gray and green,
The fresh young buttercups were seen,
And small spring-beauties, sent to be
The heralds of anemone:
All just as when I earliest heard
The cardinal bird.

The Cardinal Bird (cont'd)

Upon the gray old forest's rim
I snuffed the crab-tree's sweet perfume;
And farther, where the light was dim,
I saw the bloom
Of May-apples, beneath the tent
Of umbrel leaves above them bent;
Where oft was shifting light and shade
The blue-eyed ivy wildly strayed;
And Solomon's-seal, in graceful play,
Swung where the straggling sunlight lay:
The same as when I earliest heard
The cardinal bird.

And on the slope, above the rill
That wound among the sugar-trees,
I heard them at their labors still,
The murmuring bees:
Bold foragers! that come and go
Without permit from friend or foe;
In the tall tulip-trees o'erhead
On pollen greedily they fed,
And from low purple phlox, that grew
About my feet, sipped honey-dew: -
How like the scenes when first I heard
The cardinal bird!

How like! - and yet . . . The spell grows weak: -
Ah, but I miss the sunny brow -
The sparkling eye - the ruddy cheek!
Where, where are now
The three who then beside me stood
Like sunbeams in the dusky wood?
Alas, I am alone! Since then,
They've trod the weary ways of men:
One on the eve of manhood died;
Two in its flush of power and pride.
Their graves are green, where first we heard
The cardinal bird.

The Cardinal Bird (cont'd)

The redbird, from the window hung,
Not long my fancies thus beguiled:
Again in maple-groves it sung
Its wood-notes wild;
For, rousing with a tearful eye,
I gave it to the trees and sky:
I missed so much those brothers three,
Who walked youth's flowery ways with me,
I could not, dared not but believe
It too had brothers, that would grieve
Till in old haunts again't was heard, -
The cardinal bird.

Cat-Bird

The Cat-Bird

by Edith Matilda Thomas

He sits on a branch of yon blossoming bush,
This madcap cousin of robin and thrush,
And sings without ceasing the whole morning long!
Now wild, now tender, the wayward song
That flows from his soft gray, fluttering throat.
But often he stops in his sweetest note,
And, shaking a flower from the blossoming bough,
Drawls out, "Mi-ew, mi-ou!"

Dear merry mocker, your mimic art
Makes drowsy Grimalkin awake with a start,
And peer all around with a puzzled air -
For who would suppose that one would dare
To mimic the voice of a mortal foe!
You're safe on the bough, as well you know,
And if ever a bird could laugh, 'tis you,
Drawling, "Mi-ou, mi-ew!"

Chickadee

The Chickadee

by Ralph Waldo Emerson

Piped a tiny voice hard by,
Gay and polite, a cheerful cry,
"Chic-chicadee-dee!" Saucy note
Out of a sound heart and a merry throat,
As if it said, "Good day, good sir.
Fine afternoon, old passenger!
Happy to meet you in these places
When January brings new faces!"

42

Chickadees

by Edith Matilda Thomas

Blackcap, madcap!
Never tired of play
What's the news to-day?
"Faint-heart, faint-heart!
Winter's coming up this way;
And the winter comes to stay!"

Blackcap, madcap!
Whither will you go,
Now the storm winds blow?
"Faint-heart, faint-heart!
In the pine-boughs, thick and low,
There is shelter from the snow!"

Blackcap, madcap!
In the snow and sleet,
What have you to eat?
"Faint-heart, faint-heart.
Seeds and berries are a treat,
When the frost has made them sweet!"

Blackcap, madcap!
Other birds have flown
To a sunnier zone!
"Faint-heart, faint-heart!
When they're gone, we blackcaps own
Our white playground all alone!"

Crow

From **A Summer's Day**

by Joanna Baillie

- - - dusky crows, high swinging over head,
Upon the topmost boughs, in lordly pride,
Mix their hoarse croaking with the linnet's note.

The Song of the Carrion Crow

by Eliza Cook

My roost is the creaking gibbet's beam,
Where the murderer's bones swing bleaching;
Where the chattering chain rings back again
To the night-wind's desolate screeching.

To and fro, as the fierce gusts blow,
Merrily rocked am I;
And I note with delight the traveller's fright,
As he cowers and hastens by.

I have fluttered where secret work has been done,
Wrought with a trusty blade;
But what did I care, whether foul or fair,
If I shared the feast it made?

I plunged my beak in the marbling cheek,
I perched on the clammy brow,
And a dainty treat was that fresh meat
To the greedy Carrion Crow.

I have followed the traveller dragging on
O'er the mountains long and cold:
For I knew at last he must sink in the blast,
Though spirit was never so bold.

He fell, and slept like a fair young bride,
In his winding sheet of snow;
And quickly his breast had a table guest
In the hungry Carrion Crow.

Famine and Plague bring joy to me,
For I love the harvest they yield; -
And the fairest sight I ever see
Is the crimson battle-field.

Far and wide is my charnel range,
And rich carousel I keep,
Till back I come to my gibbet's home,
To be merrily rocked to sleep.

When the world shall be spread with tombless dead
And darkness shroud all below,
What triumph and glee to the last will be
For the sateless Carrion Crow!

46

The Crow and the Fox

by Jean de la Fontaine; translated by Edward Marsh

A crow sat perched upon an oak,
And in his beak he held a cheese.
A fox snuffed up the savory breeze,
And thus in honeyed accent spoke:
"O Prince of Crows, such grace of mien
Has never in these parts been seen.
If but your song be half as good,
You are the Phoenix of the wood!"
The crow, beside himself with pleasure,
And eager to display his voice,
Opened his beak, and dropped his treasure.
The fox was on it in a trice.
"Learn, sir," said he, "that flatterers live
On those who swallow what they say.
A cheese is not too much to give
For such a piece of sound advice."
The crow, ashamed to have been such easy prey
Swore, but too late, he shouldn't catch him twice.

Cuckoo

Ode to the Cuckoo

by Michael Bruce (or John Logan)

Hail, beauteous stranger of the grove!
Thou messenger of Spring!
Now Heaven repairs thy rural seat,
And woods thy welcome sing.

What time the daisy decks the green,
Thy certain voice we hear;
Hast thou a star to guide thy path,
Or mark the rolling year?

Delightful visitant! with thee
I hail the time of flowers,
And hear the sound of music sweet
From birds among the bowers.

The schoolboy, wandering through the wood
To pull the primrose gay,
Starts, the new voice of spring to hear,
And imitates thy lay.

What time the pea puts on the bloom,
Thou fliest thy vocal vale,
An annual guest in other lands,
Another spring to hail.

Sweet bird! thy bower is ever green,
Thy sky is ever clear;
Thou hast no sorrow in thy song,
No winter in thy year.

Oh, could I fly, I'd fly with thee!
We'd make, with joyful wing,
Our annual visit o'er the globe,
Companions of the spring.

The Cuckoo

by Gerard Manley Hopkins

Repeat that, repeat,
Cuckoo, bird, and open ear wells, heart-springs,
     delightfully sweet,
With a ballad, with a ballad, a rebound
Off trundled timber and scoops of the hillside ground,
     hollow hollow hollow ground:
The whole landscape flushes on a sudden at a sound.

To the Cuckoo

by William Wordsworth

O blithe newcomer! I have heard,
I hear thee and rejoice.
O Cuckoo! shall I call thee Bird,
Or but a wandering Voice?

While I am lying on the grass
Thy twofold shout I hear;
From hill to hill it seems to pass,
At once far off and near.

Though babbling only, to the vale,
Of sunshine and of flowers,
Thou bringest unto me a tale
Of visionary hours.

Thrice welcome, darling of the Spring!
Even yet thou art to me
No Bird, but an invisible Thing,
A voice, a mystery.

The same whom in my Schoolboy days
I listened to; that cry
Which made me look a thousand ways,
In bush, and tree, and sky.

To seek thee did I often rove
Through woods and on the green,
And thou wert still a hope, a love,
Still longed for, never seen.

And I can listen to thee yet;
Can lie upon the plain
And listen till I do beget
That golden time again.

O blessed Bird; the earth we pace
Again appears to be
An unsubstantial, faery place,
That is fit home for Thee!

Dove

The Captive Dove

by Anne Bronte

Poor restless dove, I pity thee;
And when I hear thy plaintive moan,
I mourn for thy captivity,
And in thy woes forget mine own.

To see thee stand prepared to fly,
And flap those useless wings of thine,
And gaze into the distant sky,
Would melt a harder heart than mine.

In vain - in vain ! Thou canst not rise:
Thy prison roof confines thee there;
Its slender wires delude thine eyes,
And quench thy longings with despair.

Oh, thou wert made to wander free
In sunny mead and shady grove,
And far beyond the rolling sea,
In distant climes, at will to rove!

Yet, hadst thou but one gentle mate
Thy little drooping heart to cheer,
And share with thee thy captive state,
Thou couldst be happy even there.

Yes, even there, if, listening by,
One faithful dear companion stood,
While gazing on her full bright eye,
Thou might'st forget thy native wood.

But thou, poor solitary dove,
Must make, unheard, thy joyless moan;
The heart that Nature formed to love
Must pine, neglected, and alone.

My Doves

by Elizabeth Barrett Browning

My little doves have left a nest
Upon an Indian tree,
Whose leaves fantastic take their rest
Or motion from the sea;
For, ever there the sea-winds go
With sunlit paces to and fro.

The tropic flowers looked up to it,
The tropic stars looked down,
And there my little doves did sit
With feathers softly brown,
And glittering eyes that showed their right
To general Nature's deep delight.

My little doves were ta'en away
From that glad nest of theirs,
Across an ocean rolling grey,
And tempest-clouded airs.
My little doves who lately knew
The sky and wave by warmth and blue.

And now, within the city prison
In mist and chillness pent,
With sudden upward look they listen
For sounds of past content,
For lapse of water, smell of breeze,
Or nut-fruit falling from the trees.

I Had a Dove

by John Keats

I had a dove, and the sweet dove died;
And I have thought it died of grieving;
O, what could it grieve for? Its feet were tied
With a ribbon thread of my own hand's weaving.
Sweet little red feet! why should you die?
Why would you leave me, sweet bird! Why?
You lived alone in the forest tree:
Why, pretty thing! would you not live with me?
I kissed you oft and gave you white peas;
Why not live sweetly, as in the green trees?

'As the Doves to Their Windows'

by Christina Georgina Rossetti (before 1893)

They throng from the east and the west,
The north and the south, with a song;
To golden abodes of their rest
They throng.

Eternity stretches out long:
Time, brief at its worst or its best,
Will quit them of ruin and wrong.

A rainbow aloft for their crest,
A palm for their weakness made strong:
As doves breast all winds to their nest,
They throng.

Eagle

The Eagle, the Sow, and the Cat

by Anne, Countess of Winchelsea

The Queen of Birds, t' encrease the regal stock,
Had hatch'd her young ones in a stately oak,
Whose middle part was by a cat possest,
And near the root with litter warmly drest,
A teeming Sow had made her peaceful nest.
(Thus palaces are cramm'd from roof to ground,
And animals, as various, in them found.)
When to the Sow, who no misfortune fear'd,
Puss with her fawning compliments appear'd,
Rejoicing much at her deliv'ry past,
And that she 'scap'd so well, who bred so fast.
Then ev'ry little Piglin she commends,
And likens them to all their swinish friends;
Bestows good wishes, but with sighs implies,
That some dark fears do in her bosom rise.
Such tempting flesh, she cries, will Eagles spare?
Methinks, good neighbour, you should live in care:
Since I, who bring not forth such dainty bits,
Tremble for my unpalatable chits;
And had I but foreseen, the Eagle's bed
Was in this fatal tree to have been spread;
I sooner would have kitten'd in the road,
Than made this place of danger my abode.
I heard her young ones lately cry for Pig,
And pity'd you that were so near and big.
In friendship this I secretly reveal,
Lest pettitoes should make the ensuing meal;
Or else, perhaps, yourself may be their aim,
For a Sow's paps have been a dish of fame.
No more the fad, affrighted mother hears,
But overturning all with boist'rous fears,
She from her helpless young in haste departs,
Whilst Puss ascends to practise farther arts.
The anti-chamber pass'd, she scratch'd the door;
The Eagle, ne'er alarum'd so before,
Bids her come in, and look the cause be great,
That makes her thus disturb the royal seat;
Nor think of mice and rats some pest'ring tale
Shall, in excuse of insolence, prevail.

The Eagle, the Sow, and the Cat (cont'd)

Alas! my gracious lady, quoth the Cat,
I think not of such vermin: mouse or rat
To me are tasteless grown; nor dare I stir
To use my phangs, or to expose my fur.
A foe intestine threatens all around,
And ev'n this lofty structure will confound;
A pestilential Sow, a meazled pork
On the foundation has been long at work,
Help'd by a rabble, iss'd from her womb,
Which she has foster'd in that lower room;
Who now for acorns are so madly bent,
That soon this tree must fall for their content.
I would have fetch'd some for th' unruly elves;
But 'tis the mob's delight to help themselves;
Whilst your high brood must with the meanest drop,
And steeper be their fall, as next the top;
Unless you soon to Jupiter repair,
And let him know the case demands his care.
Oh! may the trunk but stand till you come back!
But hark! already sure, I hear it crack.
Away, away -- The Eagle, all aghast,
Soars to the sky, nor falters in her haste;
Whilst crafty Puss, now o'er the eyry reigns,
Replenishing her maw with treach'rous gains.
The Sow she plunders next, and lives alone;
The Pigs, the Eaglets, and the House her own.
"Curs'd sycophants! how wretched is the fate
Of those, who know you not, till 'tis too late!"

From **Verses on the Union**

by Elijah Fenton

So when to distant vales an eagle steers,
His fierceness not disarm'd by length of years,
From his stretch'd wing he sees the feathers fly
Which bore him to his empire of the sky.

Fable IV, Series One
The Eagle and the Assembly of Animals

by John Gay (published 1728)

As Jupiter's all-seeing eye
Survey'd the worlds beneath the sky,
From this small speck of earth were sent
Murmurs and sounds of discontent;
For ev'rything alive complain'd
That he the hardest life sustain'd.

Jove calls his Eagle. At the word
Before him stands the royal bird.
The Bird, obedient, from heav'n's height
Downward directs his rapid flight;
Then cited ev'ry living thing,
To hear the mandates of his king.

Ungrateful creatures, whence arise
These murmurs which offend the skies;
Why this disorder? say the cause:
For just are Jove's eternal Laws-
Let each his discontent reveal.
To yon sour dog I first appeal.

Hard is my lot, the hound replies.
On what fleet nerves the greyhound flys!
While I with weary step and slow
O'er plains and vales and mountains go;
The morning sees my chase begun,
Nor ends it 'till the setting sun.

When (says the greyhound) I pursue,
My game is lost, or caught in view,
Beyond my sight the prey's secure:
The hound is slow but always sure.
And, had I his sagacious scent,
Jove ne'er had heard my discontent.

The lyon crav'd the foxe's art;
The fox, the lyon's force and heart;
The cock implor'd the pidgeon's flight,
Whose wings were rapid, strong and light;
The pidgeon strength of wing despis'd,
And the cock's matchless valour priz'd:
The fishes wish'd to graze the plain,
The beasts to skim beneath the main.

The Eagle and the Assembly of Animals (cont'd)

Thus, envious of another's state,
Each blam'd the partial hand of Fate.
The bird of heav'n then cry'd aloud.
Jove bids disperse the murm'ring crowd:
The God rejects your idle prayers.
Would ye, rebellious mutineers,
Entirely change your name and nature,
And be the very envy'd creature?
What, silent all, and none consent!
Be happy then, and learn content.
Nor imitate the restless mind,
And proud ambition of mankind.

The Eagle of the Blue

by Herman Melville

Aloft he guards the starry folds
Who is the brother of the star;
The bird whose joy is in the wind
Exulteth in the war.

No painted plume - a sober hue,
His beauty is his power;
That eager calm of gaze intent
Foresees the Sibyl's hour.

Austere, he crowns the swaying perch,
Flapped by the angry flag;
The hurricane from the battery sings,
But his claw has known the crag.

Amid the scream of shells, his scream
Runs shrilling; and the glare
Of eyes that brave the blinding sun
The volleyed flame can bear.

The pride of quenchless strength is his -
Strength which, though chained, avails;
The very rebel looks and thrills -
The anchored Emblem hails.

Though scarred in many a furious fray,
No deadly hurt he knew;
Well may we think his years are charmed -
The Eagle of the Blue.

The Eagle

by William Sharp (from Transcripts from Nature, 1882-1886)

Between two mighty hills a sheer
Abyss - far down in the ravine
A thread-like torrent and a screen
Of oaks: like shrubs - and one doth rear
A dry scarp'd peak above all sound
Save windy voices wailing round:

At sunrise here, in proud disdain
The eagle scans his vast domain.

On an Eagle Confined in a College Court

by Christopher Smart

Imperial bird, who wont to soar
High o'er the rolling cloud
Where Hyperborean mountains hoar
Their heads in ether shroud -
Thou servant of almighty Jove,
Who, free and swift as thought, could'st rove
To the bleak north's extremest goal;
Thou who magnanimous could'st bear
The sovereign thunderer's arms in air,
And shake thy native pole!

O cruel fate! what barbarous hand,
What more than Gothic ire,
At some fierce tyrant's dread command,
To check they daring fire,
Has placed thee in this servile cell,
Where discipline and dullness dwell,
Where genius ne'er was seen to roam;
Where every selfish soul's at rest,
Nor ever quits the carnal breast,
But lurks and sneaks at home.

Though dimmed thine eye, and clipped thy wing,
So grov'ling, once so great,
The grief-inspired Muse shall sing
In tenderest lays thy fate.
What time by thee Scholastic Pride
Takes his precise, pedantic stride,
Nor on thy misery casts a care,
The stream of love n'er from his heart
Flows out, to act fair pity's part,
But stinks and stagnates there.

Yet useful still, hold to the throng -
Hold the reflecting glass -
That not untutored at thy wrong
The passenger may pass:
Thou type of wit and sense confined,
Cramped by the oppressors of the mind,
Who study downward on the ground;
Type of the fall of Greece and Rome -
While more than mathematic gloom
Envelops all around.

The Eagle

by Alfred Tennyson

He clasps the crag with crooked hands;
Close to the sun in lonely lands,
Ringed with the azure world, he stands.

The wrinkled sea beneath him crawls;
He watches from his mountain walls,
And like a thunderbolt he falls.

Eagles

by William Wordsworth (Composed at Dunollie Castle in the Bay of Oban)

Dishonoured Rock and Ruin! that, by law
Tyrannic, keep the Bird of Jove embarred
Like a lone criminal whose life is spared.
Vexed is he, and screams loud. The last I saw
Was on the wing; stooping, he struck with awe
Man, bird and beast; then, with a consort paired,
From a bold headland, their loved eerie's guard,
Flew high above Atlantic waves, to draw
Light from the fountain of the setting sun.
Such was this Prisoner once; and, when his plumes
The sea-blast ruffles as the storm comes on,
Then, for a moment, he, in spirit resumes
His rank 'mong freeborn creatures that live free,
His power, his beauty, and his majesty.

Goldfinch

From **The Village Curate**

by The Rev. James Hurdis

I love to see the little goldfinch pluck
The groundsel's feather'd seed, and twit and twit,
And soon in bower of apple blossoms perch'd,
Trim his gay suit, and pay us with a song.
I would not hold him pris'ner for the world.

Yellow Flutterings

by John Keats

Sometimes goldfinches one by one will drop
From low hung branches; little space they stop;
But sip and twitter, and their feathers sleek;
Then off at once, as in a wanton freak:
Or perhaps, to show their black, and golden wings,
Pausing upon their yellow flutterings.

The Goldfinch

by E. P. Powell

Sweet bird! that ere the world awakes,
Sits softly singing manifold;
Sits swinging toward the golden dawn,
But hast no need to borrow sold.

Dear Goldfinch! all the world's atune;
Thy lightest note finds sweet release,
My soul and thine are full of June,
And June is full of love and peace.

Hid in the heart of yonder pine,
Thy heart-mate whispers holy rest;
Thou swingest on my window vine, -
Red roses press against thy breast.

Betwixt the walking and the work,
Between the darkness and the day,
This is the hour of native prayer, -
To live and love is now to pray.

Sing I the joy that dwells within;
Sing thou the joy that is abroad;
Sing I the hope of hither song;
Sing both the morning smile of God.

Humming-Bird

The Humming-Bird

by John Brayshaw Kaye

Rare little bird of the bower!
Bird of the musical wing,
While hiding thy head in some flower,
Softly thy green pinions sing;

Sing like the harp of Aeolus,
Hum out each murmuring note
With a charm having power to control us,
As we watch thee suspended afloat.

Sweet little cloud of vibration!
Bright little feathery fay!
Wee rainbow-hued animation,
Humming the long hours away!

Sipping the dew from the blue-bells,
Culling the sweets from the rose,
Whose heart, pearly-pink, like the sea-shell's,
Yields purest ambrosia that grows.

Hid from the dull sight of mortals,
Out of the reach of the bee,
Down through the lily's white portals
Nectar's distilling for thee.

Now at the thistle's red tassel,
Probing with needle-like bill,
Drinking a sweet dreamy wassail,
Humming thy melody still.

In the bright region of blossoms
Where the gay butterfly flaunts,
Where Nature her beauty unbosoms,
These are thy favorite haunts.

Where the wild honey-bee hovers
In the perfume-laden air,
Whither stray light-hearted lovers,
Often they meet with thee there.

Always thou dwellest 'mid beauty,
Bird of melodious wing,
To seek it's thy life's only duty,
And bask in perpetual spring.

70

The Humming-Bird

by Jones Very

Like thoughts that flit across the mind,
Leaving no lasting trace behind,
The humming-bird darts to and fro,
Comes, vanishes before we know.

While thoughts may be but airy things
That come and go on viewless wings,
Nor form nor substance e'en possess,
Nor number know, or more or less.

This leaves an image, well defined,
To be a picture of the mind;
Its tiny form and colors bright
In memory live, when lost to sight.

There oft it comes at evening's hour,
To flutter still from flower to flower;
Then vanish midst the gathering shade,
Its momentary visit paid.

Lark

Pippa's Song (from **Pippa Passes**)

by Robert Browning

The year's at the spring,
And day's at the morn;
Morning's at seven;
The hillside's dew-pearled;
The lark's on the wing;
The snail's on the thorn:
God's in His Heaven --
All's right with the world!

The Meadow-Lark

by Hamlin Garland

A brave little bird that fears not God,
A voice that breaks from the snow-wet clod
With prophecy of sunny sod,
Set thick with wind-waved golden-rod.

From the first bare clod in the raw, cold spring,
From the last bare clod, when fall winds sting,
The farm-boy hears his brave song ring,
And work for the time is a pleasant thing.

The Skylark

by James Hogg

Bird of the wilderness,
Blithesome and cumberless,
Sweet by thy matin o'er moorland and lea!
Emblem of happiness,
Blest is thy dwelling-place --
Oh to abide in the desert with thee!
Wild is thy lay and loud,
Far in the downy cloud,
Love gives it energy, love gave it birth.
Where, on thy dewy wing,
Where art thou journeying?
Thy lay is in heaven, thy love is on earth.
O'er fell and fountain sheen,
O'er moor and mountain green,
O'er the red streamer that heralds the day,
Over the cloudlet dim,
Over the rainbow's rim,
Musical cherub, soar, singing, away!
Then, when the gloaming comes,
Low in the heather blooms,
Sweet will thy welcome and bed of love be,
Emblem of happiness,
Blest is thy dwelling-place --
Oh! to abide in the desert with thee!

The Sky-Lark (A Song)

by William Shenstone, Esq.

Go, tuneful bird, that glad'st the skies,
To Daphne's window speed thy way;
And there on quivering pinions rise,
And there thy vocal art display.

And if she deign thy notes to hear,
And if she praise thy matin song,
Tell her the sounds that sooth her ear,
To Damon's native plains belong.

Tell her, in livelier plumes array'd,
The bird from Indian groves may shine;
But ask the lovely partial maid,
What are his notes compar'd to thine?

Then bid her treat yon witless beau,
And all his flaunting race with scorn;
And lend an ear to Damon's woe,
Who sings her praise, and sings forlorn.

To the Skylark

by W. Smith (Poetical Register, 1803)

Sweetest warbler of the skies,
Soon as morning's purple dyes
O'er the eastern mountains float,
Waken'd by the merry note,
Thro' the fields of yellow corn,
That Mersey's winding banks adorn,
O'er green meads I gaily pass,
And lightly brush the dewy grass.

I love to hear thy matin lay,
And warbling wild notes die away;
I love to mark thy upward flight,
And see thee lessen from my sight:
Then, ended thy sweet madrigal,
Sudden swift I see thee fall,
With weary'd wing, and beating breast,
Near thy chirping younglings' nest.

Ah! who that hears thee carol free
Those jocund notes of liberty,
And sees thee independent soar,
With gladsome wing, the blue sky o'er,
In wiry cage would thee restrain,
To pant for liberty in vain;
And see thee 'gainst thy prison grate,
Thy little wings indignant beat,
And peck and flutter round and round
Thy narrow, lonely, hated bound;
And yet not ope thy prison door,
To give thee liberty once more?

To the Skylark (cont'd)

None! none! but he whose vicious eye
The charms of nature can't enjoy;
Who dozes those sweet hours away,
When thou beginn'st thy merry lay;
And 'cause his lazy limbs refuse
To tread the meadow's morning dews,
And there thy early wild notes hear,
He keeps thee lonely prisoner.
Not such am I, sweet warbler; no,
For should thy strains as sweetly flow,
As sweetly flow, as gaily sound
Within thy prison's wiry bound,
As when thou soar'st with lover's pride,
And pour'st thy wild notes far and wide,
Yet still, depriv'd of every scene,
The yellow lawn, the meadow green,
The hawthorn bush, besprent with dew,
The skyey lake, the mountain blue,
Not half the charms thou'dst have for me,
As ranging wide at liberty.

To a Field Lark

by Selina Tarpley Williams

You dear little aeronaut, cleaving the air
With the diamond keen edge of that glittering note,
I know you have thousands and thousands to spare
In the magical depths of that prodigal throat.

Sweet spendthrift! Just toss me here one living breath
To pulsate and vibrate my measure along,
To give to it wings to soar above earth,
And make it immortal - my poor little song.

77

Linnet

The Linnet

by Robert Burns

Within the bush, her covert nest
A little linnet fondly prest;
The dew sat chilly on her breast,
Sae early in the morning.

She soon shall see her tender brood,
The pride, the pleasure of the wood,
Amang the fresh green leaves bedew'd
Awake the early morning.

To a Linnet in a Cage

by Francis Ledwidge

When Spring is in the fields that stained your wing,
And the blue distance is alive with song,
And finny quiets of the gabbling spring
Rock lilies red and long,
At dewy daybreak, I will set you free
In ferny turnings of the woodbine lane,
Where faint-voiced echoes leave and cross in glee
The hilly swollen plain.

In draughty houses you forget your tune,
The modulator of the changing hours,
You want the wide air of the moody noon,
And the slanting evening showers.
So I will loose you, and your song shall fall
When morn is white upon the dewy pane,
Across my eyelids, and my soul recall
From worlds of sleeping pain.

On Finding the Feathers of a Linnet
Scattered on the Ground, in a Solitary Walk

by James Montgomery

These little relics, hapless bird!
That strew the lonely vale,
With silent eloquence record
Thy melancholy tale.

Like Autumn's leaves, that rustle round
From every withering tree,
These plumes, dishevell'd o'er the ground,
Alone remain of thee.

Some hovering kite's rapacious maw
Hath been thy timeless grave;
No pitying eye thy murder saw,
No friend appear'd to save.

Heaven's thunder smite the guilty foe!
No: -- spare the tyrant's breath,
Till wintry winds, and famine slow,
Avenge thy cruel death.

But every feather of thy wing
Be quicken'd where it lies,
And at the soft return of spring,
A fragrant cowslip rise!

Few were thy days, thy pleasures few,
Simple and unconfined;
On sunbeams every moment flew,
Nor left a care behind.

In spring to build thy curious nest,
And woo thy merry bride,
Carol and fly, and sport and rest,
Was all thy humble pride.

Happy beyond the lot of kings,
Thy bosom knew no smart,
Till the last pang, that tore the strings
From thy dissever'd heart.

On Finding the Feathers of a Linnet...(cont'd)

When late to secret griefs a prey,
I wander'd slowly here,
Wild from the copse an artless lay,
Like magic, won mine ear.

Perhaps 'twas thy last evening song,
That exquisitely stole
In sweetest melody along,
And harmonized my soul.

Now, blithe musician! now no more
Thy mellow pipe resounds,
But jarring drums at distance roar,
And yonder howl the hounds:-

The hounds, that through the echoing wood
The panting hare pursue;
The drums, that wake the cry of blood,
-- The voice of Glory, too!

Here at my feet thy frail remains,
Unwept, unburied, lie,
Like victims on embattled plains,
Forsaken where they die.

Yet could the Muse, whose strains rehearse
Thine unregarded doom,
Enshrine thee in immortal verse,
Kings should not scorn thy tomb.

Though brief as thine my tuneful date,
When wandering near this spot,
The sad memorials of thy fate
Shall never be forgot.

While doom'd the lingering pangs to feel
Of many a nameless fear,
One truant sigh from these I'll steal,
And drop one willing tear.

From **Sing-Song**

by Christina Georgina Rossetti (before 1873)

Hear what the mournful linnets say:
'We built our nest compact and warm,
But cruel boys came round our way
And took our summerhouse by storm.

'They crushed the eggs so neatly laid;
So now we sit with drooping wing,
And watch the ruin they have made,
Too late to build, too sad to sing!

The Green Linnet

by William Wordsworth

Beneath these fruit-tree boughs, that shed
Their snow-white blossoms on my head,
With brightest sunshine round me spread
Of Spring's unclouded weather;
In this sequester'd nook how sweet
To sit upon my orchard seat!
And flowers and birds once more to greet,
My last year's friends together.

One have I mark'd, the happiest guest
In all this corner of the blest,
Hail to thee, far above the rest
In joy of voice and pinion,
Thou Linnet! in thy green array,
Presiding spirit here today,
Dost lead the revels of the May,
And this is thy dominion.

While thus before my eyes he gleams,
A brother of the leaves he seems,
When in a moment forth he teems,
His little song in gushes:
As if it pleas'd him to disdain
And mock the form which he did feign,
While he was dancing with the train
Of leaves among the bushes.

Loon

The Loon

by Alfred Billings Street

Tameless in his stately pride, along the lake of islands,
Tireless speeds the lonely loon upon his diving track; -
Emerald and gold emblazon, satin-like, his shoulder,
Ebony and pearl inlay, mosaic-like, his back.
Sailing, thus sailing, thus sails the brindled loon,
When the wave rolls black with storm, or sleeps in summer noon.

Sailing through the islands, oft he lifts his loud bravura; -
Clarion-clear it rings, and round ethereal trumpets swell; -
Upward looks the feeding deer, he sees the aiming hunter,
Up and then away, the loon has warned his comrade well.
Sailing, thus sailing, thus sails the brindled loon,
Pealing on the solitude his sounding bugle-tune.

Sacred is the loon with eye of wild and flashing crimson;
Eye that saw the Spirit Hah-wen-ne-yo through the air
Falling, faint a star - a shaft of light - a shape of splendor, -
Falling on the deep that closed that shining shape to bear.
Sailing, thus sailing, thus sailed the brindled loon,
With the grand shape falling all a-glitter from the moon.

Long before the eagle furls his pinion on the pine-top,
Long before the blue-bird gleams in sapphire through the glen,
Long before the lily blots the shoal with golden apples,
Leaves the loon his southern sun to sail the lake again.
Sailing, then sailing then sails the brindled loon,
Leading with his shouting call the Spring's awakening croon.

Long after bitter chills have pierced the windy water,
Long after Autumn dies all dolphin-like away;
Long after coat of russet dons the deer for winter,
Plies the solitary loon his cold and curdled bay.
Sailing, there sailing, there sails the brindled loon,
Till in chains no more to him the lake yields watery boon.

Magpie

From **Ode XVII of Expostulatory Odes to a Great Duke and a Little Lord**
The Pig and Magpie: A Fable

by Peter Pindar, Esq.

Cocking his tail, a saucy prig,
A Magpie hopp'd upon a Pig,
To pull some hair, forsooth, to line his nest;
And with such ease began the hair attack,
As thinking the fee simple of the back
Was by himself, and not the Pig, possest.

The Boar look'd up as thunder black to Mag,
Who, squinting down on him like an arch wag,
Inform'd Mynheer some bristles must be torn;
Then busy went to work, not nicely culling;
Got a good handsome beakfull by good pulling,
And flew without a "Thank Ye" to his thorn.

The Pig set up a dismal yelling;
Follow'd the robber to his dwelling,
Who, like a fool, had built it midst a bramble:
In manfully he sallied, full of might,
Determin'd to obtain his right.
And midst the bushes now began to scramble.

He drove the Magpie, tore his nest to rags,
And, happy on the downfall, pour'd his brags:
But ere he from the brambles came, alack!
His ears and eyes were miserably torn,
His bleeding hide in such a plight forlorn,
He could not count ten hairs upon his back.

Mocking-Bird

The Mocking-Bird

by Ednah Proctor Clarke Hayes

List to that bird! His song - what poet pens it?
Brigand of birds, he's stolen every note!
Prince though of thieves - hark! how the rascal spends it!
Pours the whole forest from one tiny throat!

Lament of a Mocking-Bird

by Frances Anne Kemble

Silence instead of thy sweet song, my bird,
Which through the darkness of my winter days
Warbling of summer sunshine still was heard;
Mute is thy song, and vacant is thy place.

The spring comes back again, the fields rejoice,
Carols of gladness ring from every tree;
But I shall hear thy wild triumphant voice
No more: my summer song has died with thee.

What didst thou sing of, O my summer bird?
The broad, bright, brimming river, whose swift sweep
And whirling eddies by the home are heard,
Rushing, resistless to the calling deep.

What didst thou sing of, thou melodious sprite?
Pine forests, with smooth russet carpets spread,
Where e'en at noonday dimly falls the light,
Through gloomy blue-green branches overhead.

What didst thou sing of, O thou jubilant soul?
Ever-fresh flowers and never-leafless trees,
Bending great ivory cups to the control
Of the soft swaying orange-scented breeze.

What didst thou sing of, thou embodied glee?
The wide wild marshes with their clashing reeds
And topaz-tinted channels, where the sea
Daily its tides of briny freshness leads.

What didst thou sing of, O thou winged voice?
Dark, bronze-leaved oaks, with silver mosses crowned,
Where thy free kindred live, love, and rejoice,
With wreaths of golden jasmine curtained round.

These didst thou sing of, spirit of delight!
From thy own radiant sky, thou quivering spark!
These thy sweet southern dreams of warmth and light,
Through the grim northern winter drear and dark.

The Mocking Bird

by Sidney Lanier

Superb and sole, upon a plumed spray
That o'er the general leafage boldly grew,
He summ'd the woods in song; or typic drew
The watch of hungry hawks, the lone dismay
Of languid doves when long their lovers stray,
And all birds' passion-plays that sprinkle dew
At morn in brake or bosky avenue.
Whate'er birds did or dreamed, this bird could say.
Then down he shot, bounced airily along
The sward, twitched in a grasshopper, made song
Midflight, perched, prinked, and to his art again.
Sweet Science, this large riddle read me plain:
How may the death of that dull insect be
The life of yon trim Shakespeare on the tree?

The Mocking-Bird

by Frank Lebby Stanton

He didn't know much music
When first he come along;
An' all the birds went wonderin'
Why he didn't sing a song.

They primped their feathers in the sun,
An' sung their sweetest notes;
An' music jest come on the run
From all their purty throats!

But still that bird was silent
In summer time an' fall;
He jest set still an' listened,
An' he wouldn't sing at all!

But one night when them songsters
Was tired out an' still,
An' the wind sighed down the valley
An' went creepin' up the hill;

When the stars was all a-tremble
In the dreamin' fields o' blue,
An' the daisy in the darkness
Felt the fallin' o' the dew, -

There come a sound o' melody
No mortal ever heard,
An' all the birds seemed singin'
From the throat o' one sweet bird!

Then the other birds went Mayin'
In a land too fur to call;
Fer there warn't no use in stayin'
When one bird could sing fer all!

The Mocking-Bird

by Henry Jerome Stockard

The name thou wearest does thee grievous wrong.
No mimic thou! That voice is thine alone!
The poets sing but strains of Shakespeare's song;
The birds, but notes of thine imperial own!

Nightingale

The Nightingale

by Mark Akenside

But hark! I hear her liquid tone.
Now, Hesper, guide my feet
Down the red marle with moss o'ergrown,
Through yon wild thicket next the plain,
Whose hawthorns choke the winding lane
Which leads to her retreat.

See the green space: on either hand
Enlarged it spreads around:
See, in the midst she takes her stand,
Where one old oak his awful shade
Extends o'er half the level mead
Enclosed in woods profound.

Hark, how through many a melting note
She now prolongs her lays:
How sweetly down the void they float!
The breeze their magic path attends:
The stars shine out: the forest bends:
The wakeful heifers gaze.

Who'er thou art whom chance may bring
To this sequestered spot,
If then the plaintive Syren sing,
O softly tread beneath her bower,
And think of heaven's disposing power,
Of man's uncertain lot.

O think, o'er all this mortal stage,
What mournful scenes arise:
What ruin waits on kingly rage:
How often virtue dwells with woe:
How many griefs from knowledge flow:
How swiftly pleasure flies.

O sacred bird, let me at eve,
Thus wandering all alone,
Thy tender counsel oft receive,
Bear witness to thy pensive airs,
And pity nature's common cares
Till I forget my own.

Impromptu: To the Nightingale

by Edward Henry Bickersteth

Songstress of the woodland glade!
Seeking silence and the shade;
Haunting night with thine unrest,
Hushing the brightest day to rest --
       Come to me.

Melancholy night-bird stay,
Charm my worldly thoughts away;
Wake my lyre! while thou dost sing,
Heavenly music round me fling --
       Come to me.

Come to me when stars are shining,
When the moon high Heaven is climbing,
When the dewdrops kiss the flowers,
Clust'ring in the silent bowers --
       Come to me.

Come to me when earth is sleeping -
Angels then their watch are keeping;
When my heart is sad and lowly,
Come, sweet night-bird, pure and holy --
       Come to me.

From **Stanzas Written by Lord Capel When He Was a Prisoner in the Tower During Cromwell's Usurpation**

Have you not heard the nightingale,
A prisoner close kept in a cage,
How she doth chaunt her woful tale
In that her narrow hermitage? -
Ev'n that her melody doth plainly prove,
Her boughs are trees, her cage a pleasant grove.

I am that bird which they combine
Thus to deprive of liberty;
And though my corpse they can confine,
Yet maugre that my soul is free: -
Tho' I'm mur'd up, yet I can chirp and sing,
Disgrace to Rebels! - Glory to my King!

My soul is free as is the ambient air
Which doth my outward parts include,
Whilst loyal thoughts do still repair
To company my solitude: -
What tho' they do with chains my body bind,
My King can only captivate my mind!

The Nightingale and Glow Worm

by William Cowper

A nightingale, that all day long
Had cheered the village with his song,
Nor yet at eve his note suspended,
Nor yet when eventide was ended,
Began to feel, as well he might,
The keen demands of appetite;
When, looking eagerly around,
He spied far off, upon the ground,
A something shining in the dark,
And knew the glow-worm by his spark;
So, stooping down from hawthorn top,
He thought to put him in his crop.
The worm, aware of his intent,
Harangued him thus, right eloquent -
"Did you admire my lamp," quoth he,
"As much as I your minstrelsy,
You would abhor to do me wrong,
As much as I to spoil your song;
For 'twas the self-same power divine,
Taught you to sing, and me to shine;
That you with music, I with light,
Might beautify and cheer the night."
The songster heard his short oration,
And warbling out his approbation,
Released him, as my story tells,
And found a supper somewhere else.

To a Nightingale

by William Drummond (Flowres of Sion, 1630)

Sweet Bird, that sing'st away the early Howres,
Of Winters past or coming void of Care,
Well pleased with Delights which Present are,
Faire Seasones, budding sprayes, sweet-smelling Flowers:
To Rocks, to Springs, to Rills, from leavy Bowres
Thou thy Creators Goodnesse dost declare,
And what deare Gifts on thee hee did not spare,
A Staine to humane sense in sinne that lowres.
What Soule can be so sicke, which by thy Songs
(Attir'd in sweetnesse) sweetly is not driven
Quite to forget Earths turmoiles, spights, and wrongs,
And lift a reverend Eye and Thought to Heaven?
Sweet Artlesse Songstarre, thou my Minde dost raise
To Ayres of Spheares, yes, and to Angels Layes.

Sonnet: To a Nightingale

by Charlotte Smith
(from **Charlotte Smith's Elegiac Sonnets and Other Essays**)

Poor melancholy bird, that all night long
Tell'st to the moon thy tale of tender woe;
From what sad cause can such sweet sorrow flow,
And whence this mournful melody of song?

Thy poet's musing fancy would translate
What mean the sounds that swell thy little breast,
When still at dewy eve thou leav'st thy nest,
Thus to the listening night to sing thy fate.

Pale Sorrow's victims wert thou once among,
Tho' now releas'd in woodlands wild to rove,
Or hast thou felt from friends some cruel wrong,
Or diedst thou martyr of disastrous love?
Ah! songstress sad! that such my lot might be,
To sigh and sing at liberty -- like thee!

The Nightingale

by Paul Verlaine; translated by Henry Taylor

Like a clamorous flock of birds in alarm,
All my memories descend and take form,
Descend through the yellow foliage of my heart
That watches its trunk of alder twist apart,
To the violet foil of the water of remorse
Which nearby runs its melancholy course,
Descend, and then the malevolent cries
Which a damp wind, rising, pacifies,
Die slowly away in the trees, and before
An instant has passed I hear nothing more,
Nothing more than the voice that sings what is lost.
Nothing more than the voice - oh, voice of a ghost! -
Of my earliest love, the voice of a bird
Who sings as he sang the first day he was heard;
And in the solemnity and pallor
Of a moon rising in sorrowful splendor,
A summer night, melancholic and heavy,
Heavy with silence and obscurity,
Lulls on the sky that a soft wind sweeps
The tree that trembles and the bird that weeps.

Owl

The Barn Owl

by Samuel Butler

While moonlight, silvering all the walls,
Through every mouldering crevice falls,
Tipping with white his powdery plume,
As shades or shifts the changing gloom;
The Owl that, watching in the barn,
Sees the mouse creeping in the corn,
Sits still and shuts his round blue eyes
As if he slept, - until he spies
The little beast within his stretch -
Then starts, - and seizes on the wretch!

The Bounty of Our Age

by Henry Farley   St. Paul's Church, 1621

To see a strange outlandish fowl,
A quaint baboon, an ape, an owl,
A dancing bear, a giant's bone,
A foolish engine move alone,
A morris dance, a puppet-play,
Mad Tom to sing a roundelay,
A woman dancing on a rope,
Bull-baiting also at the "Hope",
A rhymer's jests, a juggler's cheats,
A tumbler showing cunning feats,
Or players acting on the stage, -
There goes the bounty of our age:
But unto any pious motion
There's little coin and less devotion.

The Owl and the Pussy-Cat

by Edward Lear

The Owl and the Pussy-cat went to sea
In a beautiful pea-green boat:
They took some honey, and plenty of money
Wrapped up in a five-pound note.
The Owl looked up to the stars above,
And sang to a small guitar,
"O lovely Pussy, O Pussy, my love,
What a beautiful Pussy you are,
You are,
You are!
What a beautiful Pussy you are!"

Pussy said to the Owl, "You elegant fowl,
How charmingly sweet you sing!
Oh! let us be married; too long we have tarried;
But what shall we do for a ring?"
They sailed away, for a year and a day,
To the land where the bong-tree grows;
And there in a wood a Pigsy-wig stood,
With a ring at the end of his nose,
His nose,
His nose
With a ring at the end of his nose.

"Dear Pig, are you willing to sell for one shilling
Your ring?" Said the Piggy, "I will."
So they took it away, and were married next day
By the turkey who lives on the hill.
They dined on mince and slices of quince,
Which they ate with a runcible spoon;
And hand in hand, on the edge of the sand,
They danced by the light of the moon,
The moon,
The moon,
They danced by the light of the moon.

The Owl

by Bryan W. Procter (pseudonym Barry Cornwall)

In the hollow tree, in the old gray tower,
The spectral owl doth dwell;
Dull, hated, despised, in the sunshine hour,
But at dusk he's abroad and well!
Not a bird of the forest ever mates with him;
All mock him outright by day;
But at night, when the woods grow still and dim,
The boldest will shrink away!
O, when the night falls, and roosts the fowls,
Then, then, is the joy of the horned owl!

And the owl hath a bride, who is fond and bold,
And loveth the wood's deep gloom;
And with eyes like the shine of the moonstone cold,
She awaiteth her ghastly groom;
Not a feather she moves, not a carol she sings,
As she waits in her tree so still;
But when her heart heareth his flapping wings,
She hoots out her welcome shrill!
O, when the moon shines, and dogs do howl,
Then, then, is the joy of the horned owl!

Mourn not for the owl, nor his gloomy plight!
The owl hath his share of good:
If a prisoner he be in the broad daylight,
He is lord in the dark greenwood!
Nor lonely the bird nor his ghastly mate,
They are each unto each a pride;
Thrice fonder, perhaps, since a strange, dark fate
Hath rent them from all beside!
So, when the night falls, and dogs do howl,
Sing, ho! for the reign of the horned owl!
We know not alway
Who are kings by day,
But the king of the night is the bold brown owl!

The Owl

by Alfred Tennyson

When cats run home and light is come,
And dew is cold upon the ground,
And the far-off stream is dumb,
And the whirring sail goes round,
And the whirring sail goes round;
Alone and warming his five wits,
The white owl in the belfry sits.

When merry milkmaids click the latch,
And rarely smells the new-mown hay,
And the cock hath sung beneath the thatch
Twice or thrice his roundelay,
Twice or thrice his roundelay;
Alone and warming his five wits,
The white owl in the belfry sits.

Parrot

Lines to a Parrot

by Joanna Baillie

In these our days of sentiment
When youthful poets all lament
Some dear lost joy, some cruel maid;
Old friendship changed and faith betray'd;
The world's cold frown and every ill
That tender hearts with anguish fill;
Loathing this world and all its folly,
In lays most musical and melancholy, -
Touching a low and homely string,
May poet of a Parrot sing
With dignity uninjured? say! -
No; but a simple rhymester may.
Well then, I see thee calm and sage,
Perch'd on the summit of thy cage,
With broad, hook'd beak, and plumage green,
Changing to azure in the light,
Gay pinions tipp'd with scarlet bright,
And, strong for mischief, use or play,
Thick talons, crisp'd with silver gray. -
A gallant bird, I ween!

What courtly dame, for ball-room drest -
What garter'd lord in silken vest -
On wedding morn what country bride
With groom bedizen'd by her side -
What youngsters in their fair-day gear,
Did ever half so fine appear?
Alas! at ball, or church, or fair,
Were ne'er assembled visions rare
Of moving creatures all so gay
As in thy native woods, where day
In blazing torrid brightness play'd
Through checker'd boughs, and gently made
A ceaseless morris-dance of sheen and shade!
In those blest woods, removed from man,
Thy early being first began,
'Mid gay compeers, who, blest as thou,
Hopp'd busily from bough to bough,
Robbing each loaded branch at pleasure
Of berries, buds, and kernel'd treasure.
Then rose aloft with outspread wing,
Then stoop'd on flexile twig to swing,
Then coursed and circled through the air,
Mate chasing mate, full many a pair.

Lines to a Parrot (cont'd)

It would have set one's heart a-dancing
To've seen their varied feathers glancing,
And thought how many happy things
Creative Goodness into being brings.

But now how changed! it is thy doom
Within a wall'd and window'd room
To hold thy home, and (all forgot
The traces of thy former lot),
Clutching the wires with progress slow,
Still round and round thy cage to go;
Or cross the carpet: - alter'd case!
This now is all the daily travel's space.

Yet here thou art a cherish'd droll,
Known by the name of Pretty Poll;
Oft fed by lady's gentle hand
With sops and sugar at command,
And sometimes too a nut or cherry,
Which in thy claws to beak and eye
Thou seemst to raise right daintily,
Turning it oft, as if thou still
Wert scanning it with cautious skill
Provoking urchins near to laughter loud and merry.
See, gather'd round, a rosy band,
With eager upcast eyes they stand,
Marking thy motions and withal
Delighting on thy name to call;
And hear, like human speech, reply
Come from thy beak most curiously.
They shout, they mow, they grin, they giggle,
Clap hands, hoist arms, and shoulders wriggle;
O here, well may we say or sing,
That learning is a charming thing!
For thou, 'neeth thy wire-woven dome,
A learned creature hast become;
And hast by dint of oft repeating,
Got words by rote, the vulgar cheating,
Which, once in ten times well applied,
Are to the skies with praises cried,
So letter'd dunces oft impose
On simple fools their studied prose.

Lines to a Parrot (cont'd)

Ay o'er thy round though unwigg'd head,
Full many a circling year has sped,
Since thou kept terms within thy college,
From many tutors, short and tall,
In braid or bonnet, cap or caul,
Imbibing wondrous stores of seeming knowledge.
And rarely Bachelor of Arts
Or Master (dare we say it?) imparts
To others such undoubted pleasure
From all his stores of classic treasure:
And ladies sage, whose learned saws
To cognoscenti friends give laws,
Rarely, I trow, can so excite
A listening circle with delight,
And rarely their acquirements shine
Through such a lengthen'd course as thine.

The grannams of this group so gay,
Who round thee now their homage pay,
Belike have in such youthful glee
With admiration gazed on thee;
And yet no wrinkled line betrays
The long course of thy lengthen'd days.
Thy bark of life has kept afloat
As on a shoreless sea, where not
Or change or progress may be traced;
Time hath with thee been leaden-paced

But ah! proud beauty, on whose head
Some three-score years no blight have shed,
Untoward days will come at length,
When thou, of spirit reft and strength,
Wilt mope and pine, year after year
Which all one moulting-time appear,
And this bright plumage, dull and rusty,
Will seem neglected, shrunk and dusty,
And scarce a feather's rugged stump
Be left to grace thy fretted rump.
Mew'd in a corner of thy home,
Having but little heart to roam,
Thou'lt wink and peer -- a wayward elf
And croon and clutter to thyself,
Screaming at visitors with spite,
And opening wide thy beak to bite.

Lines to a Parrot (cont'd)

Yet in old age still wilt thou find
Some constant friend thy wants to mind,
Whose voice thou'lt know, whose hand thou'lt seek,
Turning to it thy feather'd cheek;
Grateful to her, though cross and froward
To all beside, and it will go hard
But she will love thee, e'en when life's last goal
Thou'st reach'd, and call thee still her Pretty Poll.

Now from these lines, young friends, I know
A lesson might be drawn to shew
How, like our bird, on life's vain stage,
Pass human childhood, prime and age:
But conned comparisons, I doubt,
Might put your patience to the rout,
 And all my pains small thanks receive,
 So this to wiser folks I leave.

The Parrot

by Thomas Campbell

A parrot, from the Spanish main,
Full young and early caged came o'er,
With bright wings to the bleak domain
Of Mulla's shore.

To spicy groves where he had won
His plumage of resplendent hue,
His native fruits, and skies, and sun,
He bade adieu.

For these he changed the smoke of turf,
A heathery land and misty sky,
And turned on rocks and raging surf
His golden eye.

But petted in our climate cold,
He lived and chattered many a day:
Until with age, from green and gold
His wings grew grey.

At last when blind, and seeming dumb,
He scolded, laughed, and spoke no more,
A Spanish stranger chanced to come
To Mulla's shore;

He hailed the bird in Spanish speech,
The bird in Spanish speech replied;
Flapped round the cage with joyous screech,
Dropt down, and died.

The Parrot

by James Elroy Flecker

The old professor of Zoology
Shook his long beard and spake these words to me:
"Compare the parrot with the dove. They are
In shape the same: in hue dissimilar.
The Indian bird, which may be sometimes seen
In red or black, is generally green.
His beak is very hard: it has been known
To crack thick nuts and penetrate a stone,
Alas, that when you teach him how to speak
You find his head is harder than his beak!
The passionless Malay can safely drub
The pates of parrots with an iron club:
The ingenious fowls, like boys they beat at school,
Soon learn to recognize a Despot's rule.
Now if you'd train a parrot, catch him young,
While soft the mouth and tractable the tongue.
Old birds are fools: they dodder in their speech,
More eager to forget than you to teach;
They swear one curse, then gaze at you askance,
And all oblivion thickens in their glance.

Thrice blest whose parrot of his own accord
Invents new phrases to delight his Lord,
Who spurns the dull quotidian task and tries
Selected words that prove him good and wise.

Ah, once it was my privilege to know
A bird like this ....
But that was long ago!"

Peacock

from **Truth**

by William Cowper

The self-applauding bird, the peacock, see -
Mark what a sumptuous pharisee is he!
Meridian sunbeams tempt him to unfold
His radiant glories; azure, green, and gold:
He treads as if, some solemn music near,
His measur'd step were govern'd by his ear;
And seems to say - Ye meaner fowl, give place:
I am all splendour, dignity, and grace!

The White Peacock

by William Sharp

Here where the sunlight
Floodeth the garden,
Where the pomegranate
Reareth its glory
Of gorgeous blossom;
Where the oleanders
Dream through the noontides;
And, like surf O' the sea
Round cliffs of basalt,
The thick magnolias
In billowy masses
Front the sombre green of the ilexes:
Here where the heat lies
Pale blue in the hollows,
Where blue are the shadows
On the fronds of the cactus,
Where pale blue the gleaming
Of fir and cypress,
With the cones upon them
Amber or glowing
With virgin gold:
Here where the honey-flower
Makes the heat fragrant,
As though from the gardens
Of Gulistan,
Where the bulbul singeth
Through a mist of roses,
A breath were borne:
Here where the dream-flowers,
The cream-white poppies
Silently waver,
And where the Scirocco,
Faint in the hollows,
Foldeth his soft white wings in the sunlight,
And lieth sleeping
Deep in the heart of
A sea of white violets:
Here, as the breath, as the soul of this beauty,
Moveth in silence, and dreamlike, and slowly,
White as a snow-drift in mountain valleys
When softly upon it the gold light lingerst
White as the foam O' the sea that is driven
O'er billows of azure agleam with sun-yellow:

The White Peacock (cont'd)

Cream-white and soft as the breasts of a girl,
Moves the White Peacock, as though through the noontide
A dream of the moonlight were real for a moment.
Dim on the beautiful fan that he spreadeth,
Foldeth and spreadeth abroad in the sunlight,
Dim on the cream-white are blue adumbrations,
Shadows so pale in their delicate blueness
That visions they seem as of vanishing violets,
The fragrant white violets veined with azure,
Pale, pale as the breath of blue smoke in far woodlands.
Here, as the breath, as the soul of this beauty,
White as a cloud through the heats of the noontide
Moves the White Peacock.

Robin

The Winter Robin

by Thomas Bailey Aldrich

Now is that sad time of year,
When no flower or leaf is here;
When in misty southern ways
Oriole and jay have flown,
And of all sweet birds, alone
The Robin stays.

So give thanks at Christmas-tide;
Hopes of springtime yet abide!
See, in spite of darksome days,
Wind and rain and winter chill
Snow, and sleet-hung branches, still
The Robin stays!

Robin Redbreast

by William Allingham

Good-by, good-by to summer!
For summer's nearly done;
The garden smiling faintly,
Cool breezes in the sun;
Our thrushes now are silent,
Our swallows flown away, -
But Robin's here, in coat of brown,
And ruddy breastknot gay.
Robin, Robin Redbreast,
O Robin dear!
Robin sings so sweetly
In the falling of the year.

Bright yellow, red, and orange,
The leaves come down in hosts;
The trees are Indian princes,
But soon they'll turn to ghosts;
The scanty pears and apples
Hang russet on the bough;
It's autumn, autumn, autumn late,
'Twill soon be winter now.
Robin, Robin Redbreast,
O Robin dear!
And what will this poor Robin do?
For pinching times are near.

The fireside for the cricket,
The wheat stack for the mouse,
When trembling night winds whistle
And moan all round the house;
The frosty ways like iron,
The branches plumed with snow, -
Alas! in winter dead and dark,
Where can poor Robin go?
Robin, Robin Redbreast,
O Robin dear!
And a crumb of bread for Robin,
His little heart to cheer!

The Robin in Winter

by William Cowper

No noise is here, or none that hinders thought.
The redbreast warbles still, but is content
With slender notes, and more than half suppressed:
Pleased with his solitude, and flitting light
From spray to spray, where'er he rest he shakes
From many a twig the pendent drops of ice,
That twinkle in the withered leaves below.
Stillness, accompanied with sounds so soft,
Charms more than silence.

From **The Village Curate**

by The Rev. James Hurdis

Only the solitary robin sings,
And perch'd aloft with melancholy note
Chants out the dirge of Autumn; cheerless bird,
That loves the brown and desolated scene,
And scanty fare of Winter.

Sir Robin

by Lucy Larcom

Rollicking Robin is here again,
What does he care for the April rain?
Care for it? Glad of it. Doesn't he know
That the April rain carries off the snow,
And coaxes out leaves to shadow his nest,
And washes his pretty red Easter vest,
And makes the juice of the cherry sweet,
For his hungry little robins to eat?
"Ha! ha! ha!" hear the jolly bird laugh.
"That isn't the best of the story, by half."

Gentleman Robin, he walks up and down,
Dressed in orange-tawny and black and brown.
Though his eye is so proud and his step so firm,
He can always stoop to pick up a worm.
With a twist of his head, and a strut and a hop,
To his robin-wife, in the peach treetop,
Chirping her heart out, he calls: "My dear,
You don't earn your living! Come here! Come here!
Ha! ha! ha! Life is lovely and sweet;
But what would it be if we'd nothing to eat?"

Robin, Sir Robin, gay, red-vested knight,
Now you have come to us, summer's in sight.
You never dream of the wonders you bring, -
Visions that follow the flash of your wing;
How all the beautiful by-and-by
Around you and after you seems to fly!
Sing on, or eat on, as pleases your mind!
Well have you earned every morsel you find.
"Aye! Ha! ha! ha!" whistles Robin. "My dear,
Let us all take our own choice of good cheer!"

The Redbreast

by Charles H. Luders

In country lanes the robins sing,
Clear-throated, joyous, swift of wing,
From misty dawn to dewy eve
(Though cares of nesting vex and grieve)
Their little heart-bells ring and ring.

And when the roses say to Spring:
"Your reign is o'er" when breezes bring
The scent of spray that lovers weave
In country lanes.

The redbreast still is heard to fling
His music forth; and he will cling
To Autumn till the winds bereave
Her yellowing trees, nor will he leave
Till winter finds him shivering
In country lanes.

To a Robin

by W. H. Heid, of Hoxton

Sweet bird, the leaves are with'ring fast away,
Then fear not to approach the friendly door,
Soft crumbs for thee shall oft bespread the floor,
Thy welcome visits duly to repay.

From fierce Grimalkin safe, come gambol here,
And gladly we thy confidence will heed;
Thou last and loneliest Minstrel of the year,
Like Genius, ne'er enduring vulgar meed.

While sprightlier birds, like summer friends, have fled,
And left this fading scene for other plains,
Where warmer suns a milder influence shed,
Thou com'st to cheer us with thy mellow strains;
Those the young beauties of the year engage,
Thy grateful song consoles its waning age.

122

Epitaph on a Robin Redbreast

by Samuel Rogers

Tread lightly here, for here, 'tis said,
When piping winds are hushed around,
A small note wakes from underground,
Where now his tiny bones are laid.
No more in lone or leafless groves,
With ruffled wing and faded breast,
His friendless, homeless spirit roves;
Gone to the world where birds are blest!
Where never cat glides o'er the green,
Or school-boy's giant form is seen;
But love, and joy, and smiling Spring
Inspire their little souls to sing.

The Robin

by James Thomson

The Redbreast, sacred to the household Gods,
Wisely regardful of the threat'ning sky,
In joyless fields, and thorny thickets, leaves
His shivering mates; and pays to trusted man
His annual visit. Half afraid, he first
Against the window beats; then, brisk, alights
On the warm hearth; then hopping o'er the floor,
Eyes all the smiling family askance,
And pecks, and starts, and wonders where he is;
Till, more familiar grown, the table crumbs
Attract his slender feet.

The Redbreast Chasing a Butterfly

by William Wordsworth

Can this be the bird to man so good,
That, after their bewildering,
Covered with leaves the little children
So painfully in the wood?
What ailed thee, Robin, that thou could'st pursue
A beautiful creature
That is gentle by nature?
Beneath the summer sky,
From flower to flower let him fly;
'Tis all that he wishes to do.

The cheerer thou of our indoor sadness,
He is the friend of our summer gladness;
What hinders then that ye should be
playmates in the sunny weather,
And fly about in the air together?
His beautiful wings in crimson are drest,
A crimson as bright as thine own:
If thou wouldst be happy in thy nest,
Love him, or leave him alone!

Sandpiper

The Sandpiper

by Celia Thaxter

Across the narrow beach we flit,
One little sandpiper and I,
And fast I gather, bit by bit,
The scattered driftwood bleached and dry.
The wild waves reach their hands for it,
The wild wind raves, the tide runs high,
As up and down the beach we flit, -
One little sandpiper and I.

Above our heads the sullen clouds
Scud black and swift across the sky;
Like silent ghosts in misty shrouds
Stand out the white lighthouses high.
Almost as far as eye can reach
I see the close-reefed vessels fly,
As fast we flit along the beach, -
One little sandpiper and I.

I watch him as he skims along,
Uttering his sweet and mournful cry.
He starts not at my fitful song,
Or flash of fluttering drapery.
He has no thought of any wrong;
He scans me with a fearless eye:
Staunch friends are we, well tried and strong,
The little sandpiper and I.

Comrade, where wilt thou be to-night
When the loosed storm breaks furiously?
My driftwood fire will burn so bright!
To what warm shelter canst thou fly?
I do not fear for thee, though wroth
The tempest rushes through the sky:
For are we not God's children both,
Thou, little sandpiper, and I?

Sea-Gull

Sea-Birds

by Elizabeth Akers Allen

O lonesome sea-gull, floating far
Over the ocean's icy waste,
Aimless and wide thy wanderings are,
Forever vainly seeking rest: -
Where is thy mate, and where thy nest?

'Twixt wintry sea and wintry sky,
Cleaving the keen air with thy breast,
Thou sailest slowly, solemnly;
No fetter on thy wing is pressed: -
Where is thy mate, and where thy nest?

O restless, homeless human soul,
Following for aye thy nameless quest,
The gulls float, and the billows roll;
Thou watchest still, and questionest; -
Where is thy mate, and where thy nest?

A Visit from the Sea

by Robert Louis Stevenson

Far from the loud sea beaches
Where he goes fishing and crying,
Here in the inland garden
Why is the sea-gull flying?

Here are no fish to dive for;
Here is the corn and lea;
Here are the green trees rustling.
Hie away home to sea!

Fresh is the river water
And quiet among the rushes;
This is no home for the sea-gull
But for the rooks and thrushes.

Pity the bird that has wandered!
Pity the sailor ashore!
Hurry him home to the ocean,
Let him come here no more!

High on the sea-cliff ledges
The white gulls are trooping and crying;
Here among rooks and roses,
Why is the sea-gull flying?

Sparrow

The Sparrow at Sea

by Elizabeth Akers Allen

Against the baffling winds, with slow advance,
One drear December day,
Up the vex'd Channel, tow'rd the coast of France,
Our vessel urged her way.

Around the dim horizon's misty slopes
The storm its banners hung;
And, pulling bravely at the heavy ropes,
The dripping sailors sung.

A little land-bird, from its home-nest warm,
Bewilder'd, driven, and lost,
With wearied wings, came drifting on the storm,
From the far English coast.

Blown blindly onward with a headlong speed
It could not guide or check,
Seeking some shelter in its utter need,
It dropp'd upon the deck.

Forgetting all its dread of human foes,
Desiring only rest,
It folded its weak wings, and nestled close
And gladly to my breast.

Wherefore - I said - this little flickering life,
Which now all panting lies,
Shall yet forget its peril and its strife,
And soar in sunny skies.

To-morrow, gaining England's shore again,
Its wings shall find their rest,
And soon, among the leaves of some green lane,
Brood o'er a summer nest.

And when amid my future wanderings,
My far and devious guest,
I hear a warbling bird, whose carol rings
More sweetly than the rest, -

Then I shall say, with heart awake and warm,
And sudden sympathy,
"It is the bird I shelter'd in the storm,
The life I saved at sea!"

The Sparrow at Sea (cont'd)

But when the morning fell across the ship,
And storm and cloud were fled,
The golden beak no longer sought my lip, -
The wearied bird was dead.

The bitter cold, the driving wind and rain, -
Were borne too many hours;
My pity came too late and all in vain, -
Sunshine on frozen flowers.

Thus many a heart which dwells in grief and tears,
Braving and suffering much,
Bears patiently the wrong and pain of years,
But breaks at love's first touch.

Golden Crown Sparrow of Alaska

by John Burroughs

Oh, minstrel of these borean hills,
Where twilight hours are long,
I would my boyhood's fragrant days
Had known thy plaintive song;

Had known thy vest of ashen gray,
Thy coat of drab and brown,
The bands of jet upon thy head
That clasp thy golden crown.

We heard thee in the cold White Pass,
Where cloud and mountain meet,
Again where Muir's glacier shone
Far spread beneath our feet.

I bask me now on emerald heights
To catch thy faintest strain,
But cannot tell if in thy lay
Be more of joy or pain.

Far off behold the snow-white peaks
Athwart the sea's blue-shade;
Anear there rise green Kadiak hills,
Wherein thy nest is made.

I hear the wild bee's mellow chord,
In airs that swim above;
The lesser hermit tunes his flute
To solitude and love.

But thou, sweet singer of the wild,
I give more heed to thee;
Thy wistful note of fond regret
Strikes deeper chords in me.

Farewell, dear bird! I turn my face
To other skies than thine -
A thousand leagues of land and sea
Between thy home and mine.

The English Sparrow

by Mary Isabella Forsyth

So dainty in plumage and hue,
A study in grey and in brown,
How little, how little we knew
The pest he would prove to the town!

From dawn until daylight grows dim,
Perpetual chatter and scold.
No winter migration for him,
Not even afraid of the cold!

Scarce a song-bird he fails to molest,
Belligerent, meddlesome thing!
Wherever he goes as a guest
He is sure to remain as a King.

Yet, from tip of his tail to his beak,
I like him, the sociable elf.
The reason is needless to seek, -
Because I'm a gossip myself.

The Field-Sparrow

by Lucy Larcom

A bubble of music floats
The slope of the hillside over;
A little wandering sparrow's notes;
And the bloom of yarrow and clover,
And the smell of sweet-fern and the bayberry leaf,
On his ripple of song are stealing;
For he is a chartered thief,
The wealth of the fields revealing.

One syllable, clear and soft
As a raindrop's silvery patter,
Or a tinkling fairy-bell, heard aloft,
In the midst of the merry chatter
Of robin and linnet and wren and jay, -
One syllable, oft repeated:
He has but a word to say,
And of that he will not be cheated.

The singer I have not seen;
But the song I arise and follow
The brown hills over, the pastures green,
And into the sunlit hollow.
With a joy that his life unto mine has lent,
I can feel my glad eyes glisten,
Though he hides in his happy tent,
While I stand outside, and listen.

This way would I also sing,
My dear little hillside neighbor!
A tender carol of peace to bring
To the sunburnt fields of labor
Is better than making a loud ado;
Trill on, amid clover and yarrow!
There's a heart-beat echoing you,
And blessing you, blithe little sparrow!

The Song Sparrow

by George Parsons Lathrop

Glimmers gray the leafless thicket
Close beside my garden gate,
Where, so light, from post to picket
Hops the sparrow, blithe, sedate;
Who, with meekly folded wing,
Comes to sun himself and sing.

It was there, perhaps, last year,
That this little house he built;
For he seems to perk and peer,
And to twitter, too, and tilt
The bare branches in between,
With a fond, familiar mien.

Once, I know, there was a nest,
Held there by the sideward thrust
Of those twigs that touch his breast;
Though 'tis gone now. Some rude gust
Caught it, over-full of snow, -
Bent the bush - and robbed it so.

Thus our highest holds are lost,
By the ruthless winter's wind,
When, with swift-dismantling frost,
The green woods we dwelt in, thinned
Of their leafage, grow too cold
For frail hopes of summer's mold.

But if we, with spring-days mellow,
Wake to woeful wrecks of change,
And the sparrow's ritornello
Scaling still its old sweet range;
Can we do a better thing
Than, with him, still build and sing?

Oh! my sparrow, thou dost breed
Thought in me beyond all telling;
Shootest through me sunlight, seed,
And fruitful blessing, with that welling,
Ripple of ecstatic rest,
Gurgling ever from thy breast!

The Song Sparrow (cont'd)

And thy breezy carol spurs
Vital motion in my blood,
Such as in the sapwood stirs,
Swells and shapes the pointed bud
Of the lilac; and besets
The hollows thick with violets.

Yet I know not any charm
That can make the fleeting time
Of thy sylvan, faint alarm
Suit itself to human rhyme;
And my yearning rythmic word
Does thee grievous wrong, dear bird.

So, however thou hast wrought
This wild joy on heart and brain,
It is better left untaught.
Take thou up the song again;
There is nothing sad afloat
On the tide that swells thy throat!

The Song-Sparrow

by Celia Thaxter

In this sweet, tranquil afternoon of spring,
While the low sun declines in the clear west,
I sit and hear the blithe song-sparrow sing
His strain of rapture not to be suppressed;
Pondering life's problem strange, while death draws near,
I listen to his dauntless song of cheer.

His shadow flits across the quiet stone:
Like that brief transit is my space of days;
For, like a flower's faint perfume, youth is flown
Already, and there rests on all life's ways
A dimness; closer my beloved I clasp,
For all dear things seem slipping from my grasp.

Death touches all; the light of loving eyes
Goes out in darkness, comfort is withdrawn;
Lonely, and lonelier still the pathway lies,
Going toward the fading sunset from the dawn:
Yet hark! while those fine notes the silence break,
As if all trouble were some grave mistake!

Thou little bird, how canst thou thus rejoice,
As if the world had known nor sin nor curse?
God never meant to mock us with that voice!
That is the key-note of the universe,
That song of perfect trust, of perfect cheer,
Courageous, constant, free of doubt or fear.

My little helper, ah, my comrade sweet,
My old companion in that far-off time
When on life's threshold childhood's winged feet
Danced in the sunrise! Joy was at its prime
When all my heart responded to the song,
Unconscious of earth's discords harsh and strong.

Now, grown aweary, sad with change and loss,
With the enigma of myself dismayed;
Poor, save in deep desire to bear the cross
God's hand on his defenseless creatures laid,
With patience, - here I sit this eve of spring,
And listen with bowed head, while thou dost sing.

The Song-Sparrow (cont'd)

And slowly all my soul with comfort fills,
And the old hope revives and courage grows;
Up the deserted shore a fresh tide thrills,
And like a dream the dark mood melts and goes,
And with thy joy again will I rejoice:
God never meant to mock us with that voice!

Swallow

From Scating: A Poem

by Joseph Addison, Esq.
(A translation of a Latin poem by Mr. Thomas Newcomb)

So when a swallow wantons in the air,
The Spring arriv'd, and smiling season fair;
In doubtful mazes she her flight pursues,
Now sips the stream, now drinks the fragrant Dews;
Now skims the flow'ry meadows, but to rise,
Anon more lofty, and regain her skies.
Her airy windings each with joy surveys,
Views her quick turns, and wonders as she plays.

Swallow Song

by Anna Boynton Averill

O, to feel the wild thrill of the swallow,
The wonder of the wing,
On the soft, blue billows of air to follow
The summer, and soar to sing!

To drink blue air and to feel it flowing
Through every dainty plume,
Uplifting, pillowing, bearing, blowing,
And the earth below in bloom.

Is it far to Heaven, O swallow, swallow?
The heavy hearted sings;
I watch thy flight and I long to follow,
The while I wait for wings.

The Swallow

by Abraham Cowley

Foolish prater, what dost thou
So early at my window do
With thy tuneless serenade?
Well't had been had Tereus made
Thee as dumb as Philomel;
There his knife had done but well.
In thy undiscover'd nest
Thou dost all the winter rest,
And dreamest o'er thy summer joys
Free from the stormy season's noise:
Free from th' ill thou'st done to me;
Who disturbs or seeks out thee?
Had'st thou all the charming notes
Of the wood's poetic throats,
All thy arts could never pay
What thou'st ta'en from me away.
Cruel bird, thou'st ta'en away
A dream out of my arms to-day;
A dream that ne'er must equall'd be
By all that waking eyes may see.
Thou this damage to repair
Nothing half so sweet or fair,
Nothing half so good, canst bring,
Tho' men say, thou bring'st the Spring.

The Swallow

by Sydney Dobell

Swallow, that yearly art blown round the world,
What seekest thou that never may be found?
Whither for ever sailing and to sail?
I think the gulfs have sucked thine haven down,
And thou still steerest for the vanished strand
What cheer, what cheer! oh fairy marinere
Of windy billows, sea-mew of the air?
The viewless oceans wash thee to and fro,
Spout thee to Heaven, and dive thee to the deep:
Swallow, I also seek and do not find.

From **The Village Curate**

by The Rev. James Hurdis

The chimney-haunting swallow too, my eye
And ear well pleases. I delight to see
How suddenly he skims the glassy pool,
How quaintly dips, and with a bullet's speed
Whisks by. I love to be awake, and hear
His morning song twitter'd to dawning day.
But most of all it wins my admiration,
To view the structure of this little work,
A bird's nest. Mark it well, within, without.
No tool had he that wrought, no knife to cut,
No nail to fix, no bodkin to insert,
No glue to join; his little beak was all.
And yet how neatly finish'd! What nice hand,
With ev'ry implement and means of art,
And twenty years apprenticeship to boot,
Could make me such another? Fondly then
We boast of excellence, whose noblest skill
Instinctive genius foils.

143

Shiloh a Requiem

by Herman Melville

Skimming lightly, wheeling still,
The swallows fly low
Over the field in clouded days,
The forest-field of Shiloh -
Over the field where April rain
Solaced the parched one stretched in pain
Through the pause of night
That followed the Sunday fight
Around the church of Shiloh -
The church so lone, the long-built one,
That echoed to many a parting groan
And natural prayer
Of dying foeman mingled there -
Foemen at morn, but friends at eve -
Fame or country least their care:
(What like a bullet can undeceive!)
But now they lie low,
While over them the swallows skim,
And all is hushed at Shiloh.

The Winged Worshippers
(To Two Swallows in a Church)

by Charles Sprague

Gay, guiltless pair!
What seek ye from the fields of heaven?
Ye have no need of prayer,
Ye have no sins to be forgiven.

Why perch ye here,
Where mortals to their Maker bend?
Can your pure spirits fear
The God ye never could offend?

Ye never knew
The crimes for which we come to weep.
Penance is not for you,
Bless'd wanderers of the upper deep!

To you 'tis given
To wake sweet nature's untaught lays;
Beneath the arch of heaven
To chirp away a life of praise.

Then spread each wing,
Far, far above, o'er lakes and lands,
And join the choirs that sing
In yon blue dome not rear'd with hands!

Or, if ye stay,
To note the consecrated hour,
Teach me the airy way,
And let me try your envied power!

Above the crowd
On upward wings could I but fly,
I'd bathe in yon bright cloud,
And seek the stars that gem the sky.

'Twere heaven indeed,
Through fields of trackless light to soar,
On nature's charms to feed,
And nature's own great God adore.

Song

by Celia Thaxter

O swallow, sailing lightly
The crystal deeps of blue,
With flashing wings that brightly
Glitter the sunshine through,

What sayest thou, returning
From sunny lands and fair,
That summer roses burning
Shall light the fragrant air?

That merry days thou bringest,
And gone is winter's woe, -
Is this the song thou singest?
Gay prophet, is it so?

I know all beauties follow
Swift in thy shining track,
But to my heart, O swallow,
Canst thou bring summer back?

No shaft of sunshine glorious
Shall melt my winter snows,
No kiss of June victorious
Awake for me the rose!

Thrush

Sonnet: LXXIV
On Hearing a Thrush Sing in a Morning Walk in January

by Robert Burns
(written January 25, 1793, the birthday of the author)

Sing on, sweet Thrush, upon the leafless bough;
Sing on, sweet bird, I listen to thy strain;
See aged Winter, 'mid his surly reign,
At thy blythe carol clears his furrow'd brow.

So in lone Poverty's dominion drear
Sits meek content with light unanxious heart,
Welcomes the rapid moments, bids them part,
Nor asks if they bring aught to hope or fear.

I thank thee, Author of this opening day!
Thou whose bright sun now gilds the orient skies!
Riches denied, thy boon was purer joys,
What wealth could never give nor take away!

Yet come, thou child of poverty and care;
The mite high Heaven bestowed, that mite with thee I'll share.

The Thrush

by John Clare

Within a thick and spreading hawthorn bush
That overhung a molehill large and round,
I heard, from morn to morn, a merry Thrush
Sing hymns to sunrise, while I drank the sound
With joy: - and often, an intruding guest,
I watch'd her secret toils, from day to day,
How true she warp'd the moss to form her nest,
And model'd it within with wood and clay.
And by and by, like heath-bells gilt with dew,
There lay her shining eggs as bright as flowers,
Ink-spotted-over shells of green and blue,
And there I witness'd, in the Summer hours,
A brood of nature's minstrels chirp and fly,
Glad as the sunshine and the laughing sky.

The Thrush

by James Grahame

The Thrush's song
Is varied as his plumes; and as his plumes
Blend beauteous, each with each, so run his notes
Smoothly, with many a happy rise and fall.
How prettily upon his parded breast
The vividly contrasted tints unite
To please the admiring eye; so, loud and soft,
And high and low, all in his notes combine,
In alternation sweet, to charm the ear.

A Thrush Sings

by William Ernest Henley

Deep in my gathering garden
A gallant thrush has built;
And his quaverings on the stillness
Like light made song are spilt.

They gleam, they glint, they sparkle,
They glitter along the air,
Like the song of a sunbeam netted
In a tangle of red-gold hair.

And I long, as I laugh and listen,
For the angel-hour that shall bring
My part, pre-ordained and appointed
In the miracle of Spring.

To a Thrush

by Catharine Hood

Sweet Thrush! whose wild untutor'd strain
Salutes the opening year;
Renew those melting notes again,
And sooth my ravish'd ear.

Though in no gaudy plumage drest,
With glowing colours bright;
Nor gold, nor scarlet, on thy breast,
Attracts our wond'ring sight.

Yet not the pheasant, or the jay,
Thy brothers of the grove,
Can boast superior worth to thee,
Or sooner claim our love.

How could we transient beauty prize
Above melodious art!
Their plumage may seduce our eyes,
Thy song affects our heart.

While evening spreads her shadowy veil,
With pensive steps I'll stray;
And soft on tiptoe gently steal
Beneath thy favourite tree.

The charming strain shall doubly please,
And more my bosom move;
Since Innocence attunes those lays,
Inspir'd by Joy and Love.

The Brown Thrush

by Lucy Larcom

There's a merry brown thrush sitting up in the tree,
He's singing to me! He's singing to me!
And what does he say, little girl, little boy?
"Oh, the world's running over with joy!
Don't you hear? Don't you see?
Hush! Look! In my tree,
I'm as happy as happy can be!"

And the brown thrush keeps singing, "A nest do you see,
And five eggs hid by me in the juniper tree?
Don't meddle! Don't touch, little girl, little boy,
Or the world will lose some of its joy!
Now I'm glad! Now I'm free!
And I always shall be,
If you never bring sorrow to me."

So the merry brown thrush sings away in the tree,
To you and to me, to you and to me;
And he sings all the day, little girl, little boy,
"Oh, the world's running over with joy!
But long it won't be,
Don't you know? Don't you see?
Unless we're as good as can be!"

The Song of the Thrush

by William Sharp (from **Earth's Voices**, 1884)

When the beech-trees are green in the wood-lands
And the thorns are whitened with may,
And the meadow-sweet blows and the yellow gorse blooms
I sit on a wind-waved spray,
And I sing through the livelong day
From the golden dawn till the sunset comes
      and the shadows of gloaming grey.

And I sing of the joy of the woodlands,
And the fragrance of wild-wood flowers,
And the song of the trees and the hum of the bees
In the honeysuckle bowers,
And the rustle of showers
And the voice of the west wind calling as
      through glades and green branches he scours.

When the sunset glows over the woodlands
More sweet rings my lyrical cry
With the pain of my yearning to be 'mid the burning
And beautiful colours that lie
'Midst the gold of the sun-down sky,
Where over the purple and crimson and amber
      the rose-pink cloud-curls fly.

Sweet, sweet swells my voice thro' the wood-lands,
Repetitive, marvellous, rare:
And the song-birds cease singing as my music goes ringing
And eddying echoing there,
Now wild and now debonnair,
Now fill'd with a tumult of passion that throbs
      like a pulse in the hush'd warm air!

To a Brown Thrush

by Lucy H. Walker Washington

Beautiful, beautiful, forest bird,
Dost thou tarry to sing unto me?
Gladly thy clear woodland voice is heard,
Trilling so wild and free.

Hast thou paused in thy flight, on this oaken tree,
Ere far o'er the fields thou shalt roam,
To carol a welcoming song for me,
To make brighter my western home.

Dost thou come, sweet bird, with thy cheering song,
From some feathered throng on high?
Dost thou gather the hues of thy graceful form,
From the light of a western sky?

O linger, dear bird, 'neath my window awhile,
There is power in thy mellow tone
To banish the tear, which, displaced by a smile,
Will return, if thou leav'st me alone.

Alas! thou hast flown, far away, far away;
Still my heart will remember thee long;
Remember, at parting, thou seem'dst to say,
"Gather fragments of sunshine and song."

When Lilacs Last in the Dooryard Bloom'd
Stanza Four

by Walt Whitman

In the swamp in secluded recesses,
A shy and hidden bird is warbling a song.
Solitary the thrush,
The hermit withdrawn to himself, avoiding the settlements,
Sings by himself a song.
Song of the bleeding throat,
Death's outlet song of life, (for well, dear brother, I know,
If thou wast not granted to sing thou would'st surely die.)

Vireo

To the Warbling Vireo

by Archibald Lampman

Sweet little prattler, whom the morning sun
Found singing, and this livelong summer day
Keeps warbling still: here have I dreamed away
Two bright and happy hours, that passed like one,
Lulled by thy silvery converse, just begun
And never ended. Thou dost preach to me
Sweet patience and her guest, reality,
The sense of days, and weeks, and months that run
Scarce altering in their round of happiness,
And quiet thoughts, and toils that do not kill,
And homely pastimes. Though the old distress
Loom gray above us both at times, ah, still,
Be constant to thy woodland note, sweet bird;
By me at least thou shalt be loved and heard.

Wren

The Wren

(anonymous)

The little Wren of tender mind,
To every other bird is kind;
It ne'er to mischief bends its will,
But sings and is good-humoured still.
Who'er has mixed in childish play
Must sure have heard the children say,
'The Robin and the Jenny Wren
Are God Almighty's cock and hen,'
Hence 'tis from all respect they meet,
Hence all in kindly manner treat;
For none would use with disrespect,
Whom Heaven thinks proper to protect.

Jenny Wren

by W. H. Davies

Her sight is short, she comes quite near;
A foot to me's a mile to her;
And she is known as Jenny Wren,
The smallest bird in England. When
I heard that little bird at first,
Methought her frame would surely burst
With earnest song. Oft had I seen
Her running under leaves so green,
Or in the grass when fresh and wet,
As though her wings she would forget.
And seeing this, I said to her -
"My pretty runner, you prefer
To be a thing to run unheard
Through leaves and grass, and not a bird !"
'Twas then she burst, to prove me wrong,
Into a sudden storm of song;
So very loud and earnest, I
Feared she would break her heart and die.
"Nay, nay," I laughed, "be you no thing
To run unheard, sweet scold, but sing!
O I could hear your voice near me,
Above the din in that oak tree,
When almost all the twigs on top
Had starlings chattering without stop."

Little Lady Wren

by Tom Robinson

Little Lady Wren,
Hopping from bough to bough,
Bob your tail for me,
Bob it now!

You carry it so straight
Up in the air and when
You hop from bough to bough
You bob it now and then.

Why do you bob your tail,
Hopping from bough to bough,
And will not bob it when I say,
"Bob it now!"?

The Kitty-Cat Bird

by Theodore Roethke

The Kitty-Cat Bird, he sat on a Fence.
Said the wren, your Song isn't worth ten cents.
You're a Fake, you're a Fraud, you're a Hor-rid Pretense!
--- Said the Wren to the Kitty-Cat Bird.

You've too many Tunes, and none of them Good:
I wish you would act like a bird really should,
Or stay by yourself down deep in the wood,
--- Said the Wren to the Kitty-Cat Bird.

You mew like a cat, you grate like a Jay:
You squeak like a Mouse that's lost in the Hay,
I wouldn't be You for even a day,
--- Said the Wren to the Kitty-Cat Bird.

The Kitty-Cat Bird, he moped and he cried,
Then a real cat came with a Mouth so wide,
That the Kitty-Cat Bird just hopped inside;
'At last I'm myself!' - and he up and died
--- Did the Kitty - the Kitty-Cat Bird.

You'd better not laugh; and don't say, 'Pooh!'
Until you have thought this Sad Tale through:
Be sure that whatever you are is you
--- Or you'll end like the Kitty-Cat Bird.

A Wren's Nest

by William Wordsworth

Among the dwellings framed by birds
In field or forest with nice care,
Is none that with the little Wren's
In snugness may compare.

No door the tenement requires,
And seldom needs a laboured roof;
Yet is it to the fiercest sun
Impervious, and storm-proof.

So warm, so beautiful withal,
The perfect fitness for its aim,
That to the kind by special grace
Their instinct surely came.

And when for their abodes they seek
An opportune recess,
The hermit has no finer eye
For shadowy quietness.

These find, 'mid ivied abbey-walls,
A canopy in some still nook;
Others are pent-housed by a brae
That overhangs a brook.

There to the brooding bird her mate
Warbles by fits his low clear song;
And by the busy streamlet both
Are sung to all day long.

Or in sequestered lanes they build,
Where, till the flitting bird's return,
Her eggs within the nest repose,
Like relics in an urn.

But still where general choice is good,
There is a better and a best;
And, among fairest objects, some
Are fairer than the rest;

This, one of those small builders proved
In a green covert, where, from out
The forehead of a pollard oak,
The leafy antlers sprout;

A Wren's Nest (cont'd)

For She who planned the mossy lodge,
Mistrusting her evasive skill,
Had to a Primrose looked for aid
Her wishes to fulfil.

High on the trunk's projecting brow,
And fixed in infant's span above
The budding flowers, peeped forth the nest
The prettiest of the grove!

The treasure proudly did I show
To some whose minds without disdain
Can turn to little things; but once
Looked up for it in vain:

'Tis gone - a ruthless spoiler's prey,
Who heeds not beauty, love, or song,
'Tis gone! (so seemed it) and we grieved
Indignant at the wrong.

Just three days after, passing by
In clearer light the moss-built cell
I saw, espied its shaded mouth;
And felt that all was well.

The Primrose for a veil had spread
The largest of her upright leaves;
And thus, for purposes benign,
A simple flower deceives.

Concealed from friends who might disturb
Thy quiet with no ill intent,
Secure from evil eyes and hands
On barbarous plunder bent,

Rest, Mother-bird! and when they young
Take flight, and thou art free to roam,
When withered is the guardian Flower,
And empty thy late home,

Think how ye prospered, thou and thine,
Amid the unviolated grove
Housed near the growing Primrose-tuft
In foresight, or in love.

Acknowledgement

For many pictures from <u>The Burgess Bird Book for Children,</u> by Thornton N. Burgess. With illustrations in color by Louis Agassiz Fuertes. Boston, Little, Brown, and Company, 1919.

Bibliography

I. Books consulted in the United States

Ault, Norman, ed. Seventeenth Century Lyrics from the Original Texts. Longmans, Green and Co. 1928.

Benson, Arthur C., ed. Bronte Poems: Selections from the Poetry of Charlotte, Emily, Anne and Branwell Bronte. G. P. Putnam's Sons, The Knickerbocker Press, 1915.

Bode, Carl, ed. Collected Poems. Chicago, Packard and Company, 1943.

Burroughs, John, ed. Songs of Nature. New York, McClure Phillips & Company, 1901.

Canfield, Kenneth F. Selections from French Poetry. Harvey House, Inc., 1965.

Carhart, George S. and Paul A. McGhee, comps. Magic Casements. Macmillan Company, 1954.

Cole, William, ed. The Birds and the Beasts Were There. World Publishing Company, 1963.

Collins, J. Churton, ed. A Treasury of Minor British Poetry. London and New York, Edward Arnold, 1896.

Huffard, Grace Thompson and Laura Mae Carlisle, eds., in collaboration with Helen Ferris. My Poetry Book: An Anthology of Modern Verse for Boys and Girls. Rev. ed. Holt, Rinehart and Winston, 1956.

Hutchinson, Thomas, ed. The Poetical Works of William Wordsworth. Oxford University Press, 1953.

Ingpen, Roger, ed. One Thousand Poems for Children. Selected and arranged by Elizabeth Hough Sechrist. Macrae-Smith Company, 1946.

Larcom, Lucy. The Poetical Works of Lucy Larcom. Household edition. Boston and New York, Houghton, Mifflin and Company, 1884.

Linton, W.J., ed. Poetry of America Selections from One Hundred American Poets from 1776 to 1876. London: George Bell & Sons, York Street, Covent Garden, 1878.

Magazine of Poetry: A Quarterly Review. Volume two, January - October 1890. Buffalo, New York, Charles Wells Moulton, 1890.

Magazine of Poetry: A Quarterly Review. Volume three, January - October 1891. Buffalo, New York, Charles Wells Moulton, 1891.

Bibliography

Magazine of Poetry: A Quarterly Review. Volume six, January - October 1894. Buffalo, New York, Charles Wells Moulton, 1894.

Massingham, H.J., ed. Poems About Birds: From the Middle Ages to the Present Day. E.P. Dutton and Company (printed in Great Britain), n.d.

Matthiessen, F.O., ed. The Oxford Book of American Verse. Oxford University Press, 1950.

Rossetti, Christina Georgina. Poetical Works. Macmillan and Company, Limited, St. Martin's Street, London, 1928.

Scollard, Clinton and Jessie B. Rittenhouse, comps. The Bird-Lovers' Anthology. Houghton Mifflin Company, 1930.

Sharp, William. Songs and Poems, Old and New. Duffield and Company, 1909.

Smith, William Jay, ed. Poems from France. Crowell, 1967.

Stedman, Edmund Clarence, ed. An American Anthology, 1787-1900. Selections Illustrating the Editor's Critical Review of American Poetry in the Nineteenth Century. Boston and New York, Houghton, Mifflin and Company, 1900.

Thaxter, Celia. Poems. Appledore edition. Boston and New York, Houghton Mifflin Company, 1871-1920.

Untermeyer, Louis, ed. Modern British Poetry. Mid-Century edition. Harcourt, Brace and Company, 1950.

Untermeyer, Louis, ed. Stars to Steer by. Harcourt, Brace and Company, 1941.

Untermeyer, Louis, ed. Yesterday and Today: A Comparative Anthology of Poetry. Harcourt, Brace and Company, 1926.

Van Doren, Mark and Garibaldi M. Lapolla, eds. The World's Best Poems. Albert & Charles Boni, 1929.

Williams, Sarah, comp. Through the Year with Birds and Poets. Lee and Shepard, 1900.

II. Books consulted at The British Museum in London, England

Addison, Joseph, Esq. Miscellaneous in Verse and Prose. London, E. Curll, 1725.

Annual Register of the Year 1759. London, printed for R. and J. Dodsley in Pall-Mall, 1760.

Annual Register for the Years 1784 and 1785. London, J. Dodsley in Pall-Mall, 1787.

Bibliography

Annual Register for the Year 1789. London, J. Dodsley in Pall-Mall, 1792.

Annual Register for the Year 1793. London, W. Otridge and Son.

Baillie, Joanna. The Dramatic and Poetical Works of Joanna Baillie. London, Longman, Brown, Green, and Longmans, 1851.

Baillie, Joanna. Fugitive Verses. London, Edward Moxon, Dover Street, n.d.

Bickersteth, Edward Henry. Poems and Songs. London, William Pickering, 1848.

Choice Poems and Lyrics. London, Whittaker & Co., Ave Maria Lane, 1862.

Descriptive Poetry: Being a Selection from the Best Modern Authors, Principally Having Reference to Subjects in Natural History. London, printed by and for W. Savage, Bedford Bury, 1807.

Faber, G.C., ed. The Poetical Works of John Gay. London, Oxford University Press, 1926.

Fenton, Elijah. Poetical Works. London, C. Cooke, 1816.

Gentleman's Magazine. Volume 94, July-December 1824. London, printed by John Nichols & Son, 25 Parliament Street, 1824.

Grierson, H. J. C. and G. Bullough, eds. The Oxford Book of Seventeenth Century Verse. Oxford at The Clarendon Press, 1934.

Hurdis, The Rev. James. The Village Curate and Other Poems. London, printed by C. Whittingham, 1810.

Montgomery, James. The Poetical Works. Volume two. London, printed for Longman, Rees, Orme, Brown, and Green, 1828.

Poems by Eminent Ladies. Volume two. London, printed for R. Baldwin, at The Rose, in Pater-Noster Row, 1755.

Poems by the People: Offered by the Publishers of "The People's Journal. Edinburgh, John Menzies & Company, 1869.

Poets of the Woods: Twelve Pictures of English Song Birds. London, Thomas Bosworth, Regent Street, 1853.